JANUA LINGUARUM

STUDIA MEMORIAE
NICOLAI VAN WIJK DEDICATA

edenda curat

C. H. VAN SCHOONEVELD

Indiana University

Series Minor, 169

UNDERSTANDING LANGUAGE

A Study of Theories of Language
in Linguistics and in Philosophy

by

J. M. E. MORAVCSIK

Stanford University

1975

MOUTON

THE HAGUE · PARIS

401
m831u

Printed in The Netherlands by Intercontinental Graphics, Dordrecht
77–115

to Fred Goldstein
in memoriam

PREFACE

The origins of this work lie in an essay that I wrote three years ago for Current Trends in Linguistics 12. The essay concerned the relationship between linguistics and philosophy. Since the issues dealt with in that essay have been in the forefront of much discussion during the past few years, and one has a better perspective on some of these matters by now, it did not seem inappropriate to take advantage of the kind invitation of the editor of Janua Linguarum and rethink the subject in more detail. As it is, the essay was much too sketchy to pass for a sustained philosophic argument. The main aim, however, was to raise certain problems for linguists and philosophers, to help them to see each other's concerns in clearer light, and to indicate a new way in which one can view the main tasks of these disciplines as well as their interrelatedness.

My original interest in relating linguistics and philosophy goes back to 1956 when as a graduate student I met Noam Chomsky in Cambridge. His helpful comments and correspondence over the years helped greatly in shaping my ideas. Among my teachers of those days to whom I am indebted for their influence on my views on language are Professor Quine, and the late Professor John L. Austin, though no doubt both of them would find much to disagree with and to deplore in my views.

I spent the first part of my teaching career at the University of Michigan where I learned much about the philosophy of language from Arthur Burks and Richard Cartwright. I also profited from discussions with William Alston whose views differed from mine.

In recent years at Stanford, I have had the benefit of collaboration with Dov Gabbay. I also profited from interaction with Professors Follesdal, Hintikka, and Suppes, as well as with what was at one point the "UCLA group" of Kaplan, Montague, and Partee.

Last year I had the privilege of being the colleague of Dr. Joan W. Bresnan. Her elegant work in syntax and her deep insights have caused me to rethink the relation between linguistics and philosophy in many ways.

8

Many other faculty members and students have helped me at Stanford to see things in a clearer light. Foremost among these is Fred Goldstein. He would have been one of the most outstanding members of his generation of philosophers and logicians if a tragic death had not cut his life short. I am deeply grateful for what I learned from him during that brief but precious period that he spent here at Stanford. Fred would not have approved of this essay. It does not meet his high standards of rigor, and its publication clashes with his view that only rigorous formal solutions to sharply defined problems are worth presenting. Still, I hope that this speculative material will serve as stimulus for more rigorous work and new results. After all, one of the main points of this essay is to point to more difficult but more theoretically satisfying ways of viewing work on syntax and semantics. Thus I dedicate this small volume respectfully to Fred's memory.

J. M. E. Moravcsik
November 5, 1973

TABLE OF CONTENTS

INTRODUCTION

Understanding a language is one of the most pervasive human phenomena. It is an intrinsic part of our daily lives, something that we take for granted as we make, communicate, and execute plans. Yet it is reasonable to assume that without the capacity to understand language we could do none of these things beyond a certain level of complexity.

Philosophers have a traditional interest in questioning, or being puzzled by, what people usually take for granted. This is probably one of the reasons why since the time of Socrates the phenomenon of language has been again and again the main focus of philosophical theories.

In modern times, language, like so much else, has become the object of scientific study. The program of formulating linguistics as an empirical science concerned with language raised a host of conceptual and methodological problems.

One of the reasons why linguists and philosophers encounter difficulties in clarifying what the study of language should involve has to do with a general problem that pervades all of those disciplines that involve the study of humans by humans - the problem of trying to get a proper perspective on activities and facets of life in which we are continuously involved. The understanding and use of language is, in a way, too close to us for objective study. We have a host of data, but since it permeates our lives so intimately, it is difficult to view it as data, and it is difficult to formulate clearly the hypotheses which the data should confirm or disconfirm.

The question: "What does it mean to understand a language?" invites immediately two other questions: "What does it mean to understand?" and "What is a language?" Thus the study of language and the study of the mind must be interrelated. A person who understands a language has achieved something which cannot be characterised in any revealing way without saying something about the structure of language. (Try to characterise adequately what someone who understands chess can accomplish without saying something about the rules that govern that particular game.) At the same time, attention to the difficulties of explicating the notion of understanding helps in seeing what sort of questions about the structure of language are fundamental.

The situation is well illustrated by the difficulties surrounding the everyday concepts of reading and writing. In some sense we all know what reading and writing are; yet when one asks for an adequate conceptual analysis, so crucial for empirical work on understanding these accomplishments and underlying processes, there is, currently, none forthcoming. Reading and writing are activities, and yet clearly not merely overt, purposive behaviour. They are accompanied by something as yet ill understood – under-standing. We also know that one cannot explicate what these activities consist of, nor the accompanying processes, without some account of the structure of language, that which must be understood in order for either reading or writing to take place.

It is well to focus on concepts like those of reading and writing, for this helps to narrow the class of questions concerning language that one can formulate and answer in some systematic, interrelated way. One can raise an enormous variety of questions about language. Language is used for a great diversity of purposes, it affects many different aspects of personal and interpersonal activities, it has its physical qualities in terms of sound patterns, it evokes reactions from people, etc. It is senseless to expect that there should be one unitary science that would answer all of these questions. Its analogue would be a unitary science of matter that would combine all of what we call today the natural sciences. Such gigantic systematisation is at most programmatic; certainly no science starts out with such pretensions.

Thus, as we shall see later in more detail, one of the initial tasks is to delimit the kinds of questions and concerns that linguistics as an empirical science should handle. This would leave room for a number of other sciences to work with some of the other aspects of language. The issue of relating the different sciences should be left as programmatic: at this stage of development it is too early to raise such sweeping matters of concern.

There is a problem not only about what facts linguists should deal with, but also about what will be acceptable as a theory and explanation. To say that linguistics should explain what is involved in understanding language is as vacuous as saying that it should be concerned with language. No science counts just any correlation or any generalisation as having explanatory value. In every science we aim at certain types of generalisations and are quite content to miss others. (Thus in no science does it make sense to adopt "let us not miss generalisations" as a general slogan.) As we shall see, there is considerable disagree-

ment today on the question of what types of generalisations have
explanatory value and should, therefore, be the goal of our en-
deavours.

The difficulty, encountered as one tries to find his way among
the variety of conceptions of what linguists should deal with and
what counts as an explanation, is mirrored by the difficulty one
has in attempting to survey what philosophers have said about
language. Some philosophers attempt to draw some conclusions
about the structure of reality based on the alleged structure of
language, others attempt the same as applied to the structure of
the mind, still others view the study of language as helping towards self-knowledge, while there are always those who find in
the key concepts of a science of language a fascinating field for
general conceptual analysis. In the case of linguistics, the way
out of the confusion is to distinguish several different possible
fields of scientific study and different conceptions of what an explanation is. In the case of philosophy, too, clarification is
achieved when we recognise that there are several distinct philosophical concerns, such as the ones enumerated above, that involve attention to language; nothing is gained by trying to explain
these all within one allegedly unified account. Since this study is
concerned mainly with those questions concerning which both
linguists and philosophers have relevant things to say, the more
metaphysical concerns of certain philosophies of language and
programs that involve reformulations of tasks of philosophy in
terms of studies of certain aspects of language (e.g. the positivist
program) will not be dealt with. The philosophical work to be
surveyed will consist mostly of material that is, or is thought
to be, of some relevance to work to be done in linguistics.

Still, a few general remarks about philosophical speculations
concerning language are in order. One of these is the needed
corrective to a certain popular misconception. According to this
view certain branches of twentieth century philosophy exhibit an
unusual and peculiar preoccupation with language (hence the label:
"linguistic philosophy"). Viewed in proper historical perspective
the extent to which philosophers today are concerned with language is nothing unusual. There have been several such periods
in the history of philosophy; there will be a few remarks about
one of these, below.

Second, there is an interesting asymmetry between the attitudes of philosophers towards phenomena in general that can become the object of empirical, scientific study, and their attitude
towards language. Most philosophers would hold that once a set
of empirical phenomena can be handled within a coherent scientific framework, the philosopher's task will be restricted to conceptual and methodological issues. With regard to language, however, many philosophers - if not in their programs then at least

in their practice - maintain that they have relevant and important things to say about the phenomena themselves. Presumably this asymmetry should be accompanied by some statement about the allegedly unique contributions that philosophy can make towards understanding one's own language, or some claim about the uniqueness of the study of language in general. These are matters to be taken up later in this essay. At this point we should simply note that while the so-called "philosophy of nature" turned into the philosophy of the natural sciences, once the latter reached a certain stage of development; the rise of linguistics did not have the result of turning the philosophy of language into the philosophy of linguistics.

Finally, an introduction of this sort should not lack at least a few remarks about the philosopher who was the first to suggest, by practice more than by explicit theory, some of the deepest philosophical hypotheses about natural language. Though we have no direct evidence of Socrates' teachings, a few salient features of it emerge with reasonable clarity from the indirect evidence.

One of the Socratic claims is that clarifying the meanings of some of the key terms in our language is the most important condition for clear thinking. Second, Socrates thought that knowing what we mean by a certain term is not an introspective activity; unlike our feelings or sensations, the meanings we assign to terms of our language can be discovered equally well by other people; in fact, Socrates would maintain, the discovery is likely to be facilitated by an interpersonal activity which involves the establishing of logical relations between terms, and which he called dialectic. In short, Socrates subscribed to - indeed was the first to suggest - the "no-ownership theory of meaning". Third, he believed that finding out what we mean by certain terms in our language is the key to self-knowledge. The implications of this thesis with regard to the relation of language to thought, thought to self-knowledge, the role of the nonconscious vs. the role of what is introspectively accessible - in short, the implications for philosophy, linguistics, and psychology - are deep and far-reaching. Their exploration is a task that even today we have only barely begun.

1

SOME THEORIES OF LANGUAGE IN PHILOSOPHY

1.1. Philosophers' Preoccupation with Meaning

Linguists are accustomed to viewing their subject as having
three main parts: phonology, syntax, and semantics. On the
other hand, when one surveys philosophical writings on language
it becomes apparent that the predominant concern is with questions about semantics, or simply, questions about meaning. For
example, a fairly recent useful book, designed as an introduction
to the philosophy of language (Alston 1964), devotes almost ninety
percent of its content to philosophical theories about meaning.
This lack of balance is obviously in need of some explanation.
Needless to say, an explanation is not necessarily a justification.

One of the reasons for the philosophers' preoccupation with
questions of meaning is the historical connection between these
questions and certain key issues in metaphysics, more specifically, in ontology. A traditionally crucial difference between
rival ontologies is the contrast between realism and nominalism
– in simplified form, the disagreement between those who would
argue for the existence of universals, or properties, in addition
to the existence of particular things, and those who would attempt to account for the structure of reality within a theory in
which commitments of existence are made only to particulars
(there are other varieties of theses as well, and issues about
classes are not identical with issues about properties, etc. –
we cannot go into these matters here). This debate can be re-
formulated in terms of what one allows in one's semantic theory;
certain postulates about meanings as entities turn out to be equivalent to positions with the ontology of realism, while other, more
parsimonious semantic theories are in harmony with nominalism.
Indeed, at times the traditional metaphysical debate is conceived
of as restatable in contemporary terms as the issue over the
existence and analysis of meanings, while no such links are
said to hold between ontological issues and the theoretical assumptions of syntax or phonology.

Another reason for the asymmetry of emphasis is that the

16

theoretical constructs of a semantic theory seem more problematic conceptually than the constructs of syntax or phonology. Roughly speaking, it is assumed that the rules determining acceptable sound patterns as well as the elements that these rules deal with, and the rules that determine the well-formed combinations of parts of the language (words, sentences, etc.) and the elements that these rules deal with do not force us to postulate the existence of entities whose nature is unclear, problematic, or possibly even incoherent, while a considerable number of philosophers feel that the postulation of meanings as entities will lead precisely to such a situation. In other words, many philosophers feel that while it is relatively clear what sounds are and what segments of a language are, it is far from clear what meanings are. Hence the sustained effort either to explain meanings, or to construct a theory that could "explain them away".

At least one more reason needs to be mentioned for the preoccupation with meaning, and this is the one that is most difficult to justify. Many philosophers concerned with accounting for understanding felt - and many still feel - that once we can explain the semantic component of a language, and its mastery by competent speakers, the other aspects will somehow "take care of themselves". Not surprisingly, this assumption is rarely formulated in explicit terms, and there do not seem to be any arguments supporting it in the literature. Equally unjustified is a related assumption, often made by philosophers, according to which the epistemology of semantics ("How do we know what a rule of meaning is?") is more problematic than the epistemology of syntax and phonology (e.g. "How do we know, or what is it to know, a rule of grammar?"). Later on we shall turn to the epistemological complexities of syntax and phonology, and argue that their interest as showing something about the nature of human knowledge has been considerably underrated by philosophers.

Turning now to the philosophical theories themselves, the first thing to note is that they are designed to do a number of distinct things, or, alternatively put, that they are designed as answers to a number of different problems. Some of these are variations on the theme of explaining the meaning of meaning, others attempt to provide a conceptual framework within which an empirical science of semantics could be formulated, and still others contain specific empirical hypotheses about certain fragments of natural languages such as English. (The last-mentioned type of work is best exemplified in the writings of Oxford philosophers such as Austin, Ryle, Urmson, etc.)

In this study we shall concentrate on the kind of philosophical work on meaning that lends itself to be construed either as merely a conceptual framework for an empirical semantic theory, or as such a framework together with specific proposals concerning certain fragments of English.

Even with all of this narrowing down of the scope of our study, one ought to deal with a variety of proposals, e.g. those of Wittgenstein, Austin, Grice, etc. We shall be concerned mainly with only one important tradition that is often characterised as "formal semantics", and the other alternatives will be dealt with only in the context of certain contrasts that will be drawn occasionally between them and formal semantics.

1.1.1. The Claim that the Notions of Truth and Reference are Central to the Semantics of Natural Languages

The type of semantic theory we will be concerned with has its origins in Frege, and its representatives include members of an otherwise diverse group, including Russell, Tarski, Quine, and Montague. Formal semantics as a rigorous discipline originated with Tarski, but there are certain underlying themes that his predecessors shared with him, and certain philosophical theses that are such that though they do not entail the theses of formal semantics, the notions that they develop are some of the key ones on which formal semantics is built. Two such notions are those of truth and reference. All of the philosophers in the tradition we are considering would agree that one of the key tasks of a semantic theory for natural languages is to explain the referring functions of expressions that have that role, and the conditions under which the right kinds of sentences (declaratives?) are true. This stand brings with it the claim that to understand and speak a human language essentially involves the understanding of the notions of truth and reference. Can one ascribe the understanding of a language to a person who does not know what it is for a sentence to be true or false? One might reply to this question, that although understanding what it is to refer to something and what it is for a sentence to be true or false are essential parts of our linguistic competence, many other aspects of understanding are just as essential. Language can be used in a variety of ways, and one must understand several of these ways before one can be said to be competent in the language. Thus in order to explain and defend the claim under consideration, one must explain in what sense the notion of reference is central to understanding the various parts of a language.

One way of explicating the claim is to divide it into three subclaims. One of these is that reference and truth are what is distinctive about human languages. After all, human languages are systems of communication. There are many such systems: animals and machines also use systems of communication. What, if anything, is distinctive about the human ones? For example, warning systems, as well as signals for food or the expression of desires, are used among animals. None of these by itself involves the notion of reference. An infant expressing pain by a cry, or an animal expressing desire during mating season, is not referring to pain or desire respectively. Again, an infant greeting the appearance of his mother with some appropriate sound is not yet referring to anything. Indeed, it is difficult to give clear-cut conditions that determine the stage at which a creature has mastered the notion of reference. One of the fundamental facts about reference is that it enables us to call attention to, identify, and describe objects that are not within the perceptual environment of either speaker or hearer. Thus reference has little if anything to do with ostension or ostensive teaching situations. (On how badly the importance of ostension has been overexaggerated by philosophers and psychologists, see Harrison 1972.)

Many communication systems are conditioned by what is perceptually present to the speaker or the hearer, or both. One way to bring out the importance of the notion of reference is to point out that one cannot attribute the competence of reference to a person unless that person shows evidence of using and understanding reference to entities that are not perceptually present to either speaker or hearer.

One version of the distinctiveness thesis – and one to which certainly not everyone in this tradition would agree – maintains that there can be <u>no causal analysis of referring</u>. We saw already above, that referring cannot be analysed as an object causing the speaker to utter certain sounds. Of course, some might reply that this simple-minded account would need qualifications and elaboration. The thesis under consideration would deny that any elaboration would ever by successful. The claim that reference can not be given a causal analysis is linked at times to the claim that reference requires <u>intentionality</u>. (One would then have to defend the claim that intentional phenomena cannot be given full causal analysis.) With this version of the view under discussion, one could not attribute the ability to refer or to understand reference to any creature unless one could also attribute to the creature intentions, in fact, intentions of specific kinds. Needless to say, it would require a separate book to examine these claims and the arguments that have been advanced for and against them. Perhaps the mere pointing out of what phenomena reference is connected with and what kinds of analyses it is felt to be resisting will give one an appreciation of why this notion is regarded as so crucial in a semantic theory of a human language.

The above said apply also to the notion of truth; indeed, the notions of truth, reference, naming, and predicating seem to be conceptually interrelated, and equally fundamental. To apply a predicate involves the notion of applying a predicate truly – applying it to those things of which it is true. This same notion of application, the link between language and reality, is involved in the notion of reference. All three of these notions are crucial for understanding how language is linked to reality in the case of human languages, and these links make it possible to have this relation of language and reality represented in thought. Thus the insistence that these are the distinctive notions of a semantic theory for natural languages is not unrelated to the traditional notion that what distinguishes humans from other creatures is thinking ("man is a res cogitans"). One might go as far as to claim that making the notions of reference, truth, and predication fundamental in a semantic theory for natural languages is simply to carry out for semantics the consequences of the view that the distinguishing mark of the human race is thought.

It will be argued below that this claim cannot be taken in isolation from grammar. For, as we will see, there can be no reference, predication, and truth in a communication system without syntax. Thus the notion of grammar comes in with these semantic notions on the ground floor, so to say.

The second subclaim of centrality rests on the uniqueness or indefinability of the key notions of truth and reference. That is to say, philosophers working in this tradition would agree that the notions of truth, satisfaction (i.e. of a predicate by some entity), and reference cannot be defined in terms of some other, more fundamental, set of notions. As we will see, Tarski believes that in an ingenious way one can give truth definitions to fragments of language of certain types, but that project does not conflict with the point made here: those definitions do not reduce the notions of truth or reference to some other set of notions. As we shall see, while truth and reference are simple, indefinable terms, they are needed when one wants to give adequate accounts of the more complex notions, such as various types of equivalences, invoked in semantic theories.

The third subclaim of centrality concerns the fact that reference and truth are fundamental to a semantic theory. This fundamentality can be brought out by pointing out that while the notion of reference can be explained without bringing in various other uses of language, the adequate accounts of the other uses of natural languages do rely on the notion of reference.

What would it be like to deny the claim we are considering? For example, one might argue that we perform a variety of acts by the use of language (we perform what Professor J. Austin used to call illocutionary acts), or that we participate in a variety of what Wittgenstein called language games, and that acts of referring, or the referring uses of language, are no more fundamental to the different language games or illocutionary acts than any other use or act. With regard to truth, one might say that this is only one dimension of assessment, namely from the point of view of veracity. There are many other dimensions of assessment - why regard this one as more fundamental than the others? One could strengthen this position by adding that this sort of stand concerning the lack of central role of reference could be maintained even if we restricted ourselves to those acts and language games that are distinctive of human languages, i.e. only agents with intentions could perform them or partake in them. Surely there are many such acts and uses and dimensions of assessment; truth and reference are not the only ones.

In reply, let us consider, as an illustration, the notion of a command, and the kind of dependency that is being argued for here. To start with, obeying a command is not even an intentional act: we can train animals to obey commands. It might be argued, however, that giving commands is an intentional act. Yet, one can imagine situations wherein simple commands are given and obeyed in which the agents involved need not have or use the notion of reference. But at a certain level of complexity one must have the notion of reference, truth, etc., if one is to be able to interpret a command (and obviously, this is a requirement for giving a command - a person who gives a command that he cannot understand is merely parroting what someone else trained him to say).

In short, there are various uses of language: we can question, advise, command, implore, etc., by using language. At a certain level of complexity these uses will embody thoughts, i.e. that which can be true or false of various things. Thus for interpreting the various uses of language at this level we must have prior understanding of the notions we have been discussing.

The dependency does not hold the other way around. One does not have to know what it is to promise, command, advise, etc., in order to interpret reference and master its use. This does not mean that one should characterise the use of human languages as mere articulation of thought; rather, the articulation of thought should be held to be central to all other activities involving the human use of language, and the notions of reference and truth are essential in order for us to explain what it is to articulate thoughts in language.

These considerations should explain why many philosophers from Plato to Frege have held naming and referring to be central semantic notions. Such a view does not amount to treating all aspects of semantics as naming, or somehow assuming that all relations between language and reality can be reduced to that of naming. Thus, as we shall see below, though there are several different conceptions of formal semantics, the tradition that is being reviewed here would insist that the analysis of the semantics of the language of a rational being must have the notions of truth and reference as its central concerns, since without these notions one cannot understand what it is to use language in order to express thoughts.

1.1.2. A Central Claim in Frege's Theory of Language

We have seen so far one of the distinctive features of the semantics of natural languages, namely that it has as essential ingredients conditions of reference and truth. We now turn to another claim concerning a distinctive feature found in its earliest
and clearest form in the writings of Frege (1892: esp. 56 ff.).
The claim can be summarised as the following:

a large number of sentences of a natural language can be understood by a competent speaker-hearer without knowing who said
the sentence, where, when, why, etc.

In other words, language - to a large extent - speaks for itself:
the interpretation of many sentences is independent of knowledge
of extralinguistic context. Furthermore, this is taken to be one
of the fundamental facts about human languages, and an adequate
semantic theory has to address itself to it.

   We shall see how this insight influenced the development of
semantic theories. Until recently, it led logicians and philosophers to concentrate heavily on those fragments of English that
do not contain indexical expressions (or "deictic terms" as the
linguists call these), in short, personal pronouns or words like
here and now that need to be interpreted in each instance in terms
of the spatiotemporal locations of the speaker and the hearer.

   Let us contrast this Fregean insight with other views about
language. Only through such contrasts can one really appreciate
the depth of the insight that Frege achieved, and the crucial significance that this insight has for the study of the semantics of
natural languages.

   One consequence of Frege's insight is that language cannot be
viewed merely as a communication system. Yet such a view is
influential in the current work that aims at simulating human
linguistic competence. Consider the following: "...language is a
system that enables to communicate ideas from speaker to
hearer" (Winograd 1971:18). This general conception leads
people to conceive of the task of a semantic theory - be it simu-
lation or some other type of theory - as that of accounting for
how one person can convey something to another person. In
Frege's view this is clearly not enough: the task has been accomplished successfully only if an explanation has been given for
how a part of a language is understood, not merely as a message
from one person to another, but as an articulation of something
that can be assessed as true or false, without knowing who, where,
when, why, etc., sent it as a message, in short, without taking
it as a message.

   It follows from Frege's view that there must be a set of rules
that assign meaning to parts of a language without reference to
the intentions or circumstances of the agents involved in the

communication process. Thus the task of an adequate semantic
theory is not only to explain how communication is possible, but
to devise a set of rules that are adequate to account for semantic
data (more on that below) and meet the condition mentioned above.

   Another contrast bringing out the significance of Frege's insight involves looking at certain recent development in semantic
theory, particularly those associated with the work of Kaplan
(1973) and Kripke (1971). We saw above, that Frege's thesis required the qualification "a large part"; the claim does not cover
all of a natural language like English, nor even all declarative
sentences. Frege recognised the presence of indexicals, and
was aware of the fact that the interpretation of sentences containing those requires knowledge of extralinguistic circumstances.
Thus we can talk about a "Fregean core" in a language, and contrast it with the other, context-sensitive part. The recent work
referred to above raises the question: where shall we draw the
line? Frege's own position seems to have been that only sentences
with pronouns and indexicals are context sensitive in the sense
explained above. Recent work by Kaplan, Kripke, and others
suggests that the "Fregean core" is much smaller and the context-sensitive part much larger than has been traditionally assumed. Specifically, it is claimed that sentences containing ordinary proper names will be outside the Fregean core, since,
according to these philosophers, the interpretation of these requires knowledge of the circumstances (maybe also the intentions,
as Donnellan 1966 might claim) of some speaker or "name giver".
Kripke has even claimed that all terms designating species or
natural kinds are affected by the same context sensitivity. If this
is correct, then all sentences containing these terms will be outside of the Fregean core.

   From this brief review, the following two points emerge. First,
the decision as to which parts of language have semantic interpretations that fulfill the Fregean requirement is a crucial question
for current work in semantic theory, whether it is done by linguists
or philosophers. Second, the question of how much is to be included in the Fregean core is distinct from the issue of the existence of this core. Even if only those sentences qualify that contain only abstract singular terms, no indexicals, and no general
terms that stand for natural kinds, it is still important to recognise that there is a segment of natural languages that does qualify,
and that one of the main tasks of an adequate semantic theory is
to explain - not to ignore and not merely to take for granted -
this aspect of linguistic competence.

1.1.3. Sense and Reference, Meaning and Denotation

We have so far uncovered two conditions of adequacy for the semantic rules of a natural language. One of these is the fixedness,

or extralinguistic context independence, and the other is the function of parts of language which enable us to refer to elements of reality and to formulate things that can be true or false. These conditions suggest that at the core of semantics there should be rules that relate different types of elements of language to reality. Specifically, we should have correlations between singular terms and what they denote or refer to (e.g. the fastest man in Europe denotes the fastest man in Europe), between predicates and what they can be truly applied to (e.g. man denotes the class of all men), and between sentences and what makes the true ones true.

Giving such assignments can be called an interpretation of the language. Such interpretations give us certain equivalences; two terms are equivalent if and only if they denote the same things. We can call the denotations of the expressions their extensions; thus we get certain extensional equivalences and an extensional analysis of a language.

One can imagine languages that are wholly extensional, but it is not clear that natural languages would belong to that class. In fact, below we shall review parts of natural languages that resist such analyses, i.e. that create contexts within which the kinds of substitutions described above do not preserve truth value. But it is important to note that there are reasons, apart from the existence of these nonextensional fragments, for introducing notions other than those of denotation and truth.

The semantic analysis described briefly and roughly above can be called an interpretation of a language. But giving an interpretation of a language is not the same as giving an account of the linguistic competence of one who mastered that language. In order to accomplish that task, we have to characterise what it is that one knows when one knows the denotations of the various parts of a language. In short, the question Frege asks is: what connects a term with its denotation range? The relation cannot be a direct one, otherwise in order to understand a term one would have to be acquainted with its entire range of application. This is in most cases impossible since such ranges, linked to many predicates, are spatiotemporally unbounded. Thus the relation between term and denotation range or extension must be mediated by something, something the grasp of which enables us to say what does fall and what would fall within the extension of a given term. This element has to be the mode of representation of the extension, and it is called the sense of the term. The senses of the expressions contained in a sentence make up the thought expressed by that sentence.

The Fregean notion of sense developed into what philosophers and linguists call the meaning of expressions. We shall not trace here the differences between the various accounts of sense or meaning (differences between the systems of, e.g. Frege, Carnap, and Church). Indeed, the condensed sketch given above already mixes ingredients from various analyses, and - e.g. by not distinguishing the role of <u>man</u> from <u>is a man</u> - does not pretend to be a historically accurate presentation of the details of Frege's views. But hopefully enough has been said to show how Frege is led to talk about meaning as a result of his reflections, not only about fragments that resist extensional analysis, but about general linguistic competence and the role of reference within that.

Thus to know the meaning of a predicate expression is to know to what entities it truly applies. One has to add, of course, <u>under idealised conditions</u>. Linguists are already familiar with the competence-performance distinction that Chomsky has invoked in order to clarify what we mean by the mastery of the rules of syntax of a natural language. It is equally important to keep in mind that a Fregean theory of semantics for natural languages is also a competence theory. It does not say that if we understand a language then we can in fact pick out successfully all of those entities that fall under a certain predicate. There may be a variety of factors that prevent us from doing so, e.g. ignorance of nonlinguistic empirical facts linked to some particular situation in which the speaker finds himself, limitations of the perceptual apparatus, limitations on memory span, life span, etc. Thus it is a misconception to demand that a Fregean or any other adequate theory of semantics should tell us what we actually do when we refer successfully or when we apply a predicate truly to certain entities. Nevertheless, as in syntax, an adequate performance theory will have to incorporate a competence theory as well. At present, neither linguists nor philosophers - or anyone in any of the other social sciences - has even the faint beginnings of a theory of performance for semantic ability. Indeed, until we have a clearer picture of a theory of competence, it is unlikely that any deep hypotheses about performance could even be formulated.

What we have done in this section is to show how the notion of meaning is introduced and how it is tied to reference. These matters have so far not been given adequate attention in the literature of linguistics; in fact, there is a great deal of confusion surrounding the notions of meaning and reference. In the earlier transformational literature the mistaken notion was entertained that one could have a theory of meaning without a theory of reference. (For an attempted historical reconstruction of how this view came about, see the earlier version of this work in <u>Current Trends in Linguistics</u> 12.)

In Fodor and Katz (1963) it is rightly pointed out that linguists are interested in notions with which a mere theory of reference cannot deal. For example, linguists are concerned with relations of synonymy, and the extensional equivalences that a theory of reference gives will not yield the required relations. Further, man and featherless biped may be in fact coextensive terms, since it seems that they pick out the same class of actual entities, but they are not synonyms; thus a relation that holds between pairs like vixen and female fox must be stronger, and thus need be explicated in terms of additional notions. Similar considerations hold for a notion like that of ambiguity.

Fodor and Katz, however, failed to note the following points. First, a theory that does not give an explanation of the ability of a normal speaker-hearer to attach the proper extensions to the relevant parts of a language cannot be an adequate account of linguistic competence since it is missing a central part of that competence. Second, there is a need for saying something about how meanings are introduced into the theoretical framework, what they are, etc. There is no such account in their work, and this is apparently partly due to their failure to note that there is such an attempt made in Frege. Furthermore, as we saw, the attempt is made by invoking the notion of sense to explain something about our ability to assign extensions to terms. Thus for Frege the notions of sense and reference are intimately interrelated: there is no independent introduction of the notion of meaning apart from considerations about our ability to refer and to assign truth and falsity to certain sentences.

It seems, then, that in order to present an adequate theory of the semantics of a natural language we must assign both sense and denotation to the relevant parts of that language. We shall see in the next part of this survey various ways in which this might be rigorously and formally done.

Prior to embarking on that project, we must briefly survey certain sceptical arguments that have been advanced against a theory that would include a theory of meaning as a component. These objections have been presented most prominently in Quine (1953 and 1960). One set of objections charges the theory of meaning with vacuousness: on the one hand, it is claimed that the notion of meaning can be explained only in terms of a limited set of other notions such as analyticity, necessity, truth by stipulation, etc., and that these notions form a small circle; on the other hand, apart from the question of definability, there is not enough that we can say about this family of notions independently of their alleged explanatory role to save from vacuousness the explanations offered in terms of them. The other set of objections are epistemological in nature: they are concerned with the issue of what empirical evidence would count for or against hypotheses about meaning relations in natural languages. These objections culminate in the thesis of the indeterminacy of translation. This thesis states that, given certain conceptions of what counts as empirical evidence, hypotheses about translations are in principle underdetermined by any possible empirical evidence; thus no rational choice between certain sets of conflicting ones is possible. It is important to emphasise the double indetermin-acy that Quine assigns to hypotheses about translation. Scientists and philosophers have held for some time that given a set of empirical data it is possible in principle to have conflicting theories accounting for them equally well. Quine claims that hypotheses about translation suffer from double indeterminacy; they must be related to certain hypotheses about physical objects and behaviour. Thus they are underdetermined, first, in so far as the hypotheses about material things and behaviour on which they depend are underdetermined, and, second, because they are under-determined in relation to these hypotheses about matter and behaviour on which they depend.

Thus the indeterminacy that Quine complains about is not merely that which affects all theories in the natural sciences in general. Whether the charge is deserved is an issue of lively controversy today, much of which is unfortunately marred by the failure of linguists and philosophers to understand the unique kind of indeterminacy that Quine claims to be affecting theories of translation. In order to settle this issue, we shall have to ar-rive at a clearer conception than what we now have both of what counts as empirical evidence relevant to theories of language and how hypotheses about linguistic competence are related to - are dependent on? - hypotheses about matter and behaviour. (As an additional difficulty we have the problem that there is no clear account available of what counts as behaviour.)

As to the other issue, Quine's charge of circularity is acknowl-edged already by Brentano's thesis - the thesis of intentionality - according to which no reductionistic account of these notions is possible. The question then arises: is there a way to link this circle of notions to some aspect of experience? An answer to this question requires careful study of the claims of phenomeno-ology.

There is an aspect of Quine's complaint about the "circle" of intensional notions that requires separate treatment. Quine deals with these matters as if we had a number of well-established notions, namely those required for extensional analysis, and then a small circle of mysterious intensional notions. But it can be urged that instead of one, we have really two circles. The set of notions required for extensional analysis form a circle not wider or less mysterious than the circle of intensional no-tions. Each member of both circles can be explained only in terms of the rest of the respective circles, and the circles them-selves can only be explained by contrasting them with each other. Thus from the definitional point of view, meaning is no more mysterious than reference, and the fact that these fundamental semantic notions cannot be explained in terms of notions outside of linguistics presents us with a situation that is encountered in many other sciences as well. Why think that all sciences can be reduced to one? (This position is urged in Moravcsik 1965.)

1.2. Formal Semantics

So far we have examined certain general assumptions underlying a particular philosophical tradition in semantics. From these a specific conception of the task of formal semantics emerges: to formulate a set of rules that assigns the appropriate senses and denotation to the various parts of a language, that explicates the conditions under which the various sentences would be true, and that explains how the smaller elements within complexes contribute to the sense and denotation of the complexes themselves. We call this formal semantics because it is assumed that these rules of a language can be given a completely explicit and rigorous formulation.

Assigning to a linguistic element a sense and denotation involves correlating it with a semantic object, i.e. some extra-linguistic element of reality. In the tradition that we are sketching here, it is usually assumed that these elements will be set-theoretical elements, i.e. individuals, or sets, or functions, etc. This is why at times this approach is called set-theoretic semantics.

How does one proceed to accomplish this task? In theory, it would be possible to take the elements of language, e.g. words, morphemes, etc., one by one, and assign these an appropriate object. This would lead to enormous complications and to missing important generalisations concerning the similarity among the semantic objects assigned to elements that belong to the same category. Besides, even on such an account, some minimal, initial, segmentation would have to be assumed in order to determine what the basic units are to which the semantic objects should be correlated.

Thus formal semantics proceeds by determining what the basic syntactic categories are to which simple expressions belong, and then devising formation rules, or rules of concatenation, that show how one can combine elements to form well-formed complexes. (And since there is no nonarbitrary criterion that would limit the length of certain parts of a natural language, we have to be able to generate infinite sequences; thus some of the rules will have to be recursive.) Having formulated the syntax, we then assign to each syntactic category a certain type of semantic object, and then proceed to make the assignments within the categories, thus giving an interpretation of the language. Again, we

need to lay down rules that determine how the semantic objects
of the complexes are built up from those of the simples, and
since we can iterate certain constructions arbitrarily - e.g. con-
junction or disjunction - the rules will have to be recursive.

In an oversimplified version, one might assign to the syntactic
category of proper names individuals as their denotata; thus <u>John</u>
denotes John, etc. Again, common nouns could be assigned
classes as their denotata, thus <u>man</u> has as its denotation the
class of men. Within a more formal presentation we would introduce the notion of <u>satisfaction</u>, and say that certain elements,
i.e. men, satisfy the predicate <u>is a man</u> (and since there are also two- and three-place, etc., predicates in English, and we
want uniformity in our rules, we introduce the notion of <u>sequences</u>
satisfying predicates).

The basic notion is that of satisfaction; Tarski has shown how
one can explicate the truth conditions for sentences via the help
of this notion. The problem of stating conditions for truth runs
into certain well-known paradoxes from which there are various
ways out. (For readable and more careful expositions, see Quine
1970 and Rogers 1963; the basic paper in this field is Tarski
1934.)

Even from this informal and sketchy introduction, certain important truths emerge that need be kept in sight if and when this
apparatus is to be employed in linguistics.

First, it is fashionable in linguistics to talk about "semantic
representation", but it should be clear from the above that within
formal semantics it makes no sense to talk about "pure semantic
representation". Semantic representation is relative to some
segmentation, i.e. some syntactic structure. A decision whether
to regard proper names as constants or predicates will give them
different syntactic status, and thus different semantic interpretation. We shall return to this "myth of pure semantic representation" later on.

Second, within this framework it makes no sense to suggest
that syntax and semantics are not distinct, and it is simply not
a problem to separate the two. The rules of syntax tell you how
to combine elements of language to make well-formed sequences,
the rules of semantics associate elements of language with elements of extralinguistic reality. The two sets of rules have
different domains. Rules that show how to form complex noun
phrases out of nouns and adjectives are grammatical rules,
while rules that assign semantic objects to noun phrases and
show how these objects are related to the semantic objects
correlated with the parts of the noun phrase are semantic rules.

This clarity of the elucidation and distinction of basic types of
rules already recommends this way of doing semantics over
alternatives; later on we shall compare the clarity of this system

29

with the confusion and misunderstanding that surrounds the distinction between syntax and semantics in linguistics.

Nevertheless, we cannot regard all of the issues in connection
with which linguists raised questions about the relation of syntax
to semantics and the possible interrelatedness of these, as pseudo-
issues. Later on an attempt will be made to restate some of the
issues within a clearer and more rigorous framework.

Although formal semantics deals with the kinds of rules that
were characterised above, there are no inherent difficulties in
adding to such a system other rules, e.g. rules that explain what
illocutionary acts (e.g. advise, promise, etc.) can be performed
by certain types of sentences, or rules that have to do with emphasis.

1.2.1. First Order Predicate Calculus and the Semantics of Natural Languages

In Quine (1970), we encounter a careful presentation of what
Quine calls "logical grammar", and the corresponding semantics. The basic elements of the syntax are the following: predicate letters, variables, truth-functional connectives (including
negation), and quantifiers. (If one had a different view of names
than Quine's reductionistic outlook, one would include a category
of constants as well.) Out of these elements, with the help of formation rules, we can build open sentences (i.e. those in which
some variables are unbound) and closed sentences (that can thus
be assessed as true or false). Again, with the help of the connectives, we can form sentences of these two types of various
degrees of complexity. And since we have no nonarbitrary limit
on the number of variables or on the number of places that a
predicate can have (monadic, dyadic, triadic, ... etc.), we are
also able to do likewise for sentences of considerable quantifi-
cational complexity.

Subsequently the semantics is explained by showing how one
can determine satisfaction relations for open sentences of various types of complexity, and then define truth for the closed sentences.

The language that is sketched here is essentially that of the
first-order predicate calculus. Again, one might want to add
identity, but this brings with it other issues whose complexity
need not concern us here. (They are sketched in Quine 1970:61-
64.) The relation of this system to a natural language is that within this system we can account for what are truths of logic, and
also for a large variety of inference patterns that, one feels,
are expressed in natural languages and that would be regarded
as valid by our rational intuitions. It is worth noting that this is
all that logicians ever claimed; the logical structure expressed
within this system represents an abstraction (or "regimentation"

as some logicians call it) from the semantics of natural languages in order to bring out this inferential network and tautologies.

Recently, however, the idea has been entertained by some philosophers that this system might provide an adequate semantics for natural languages – with some minimal additions (see the writings of D. Davidson and G. Harman, for example). Thus it is worthwhile to compare the semantics of this system with that of a natural language. Such a comparison must include a comparison of the respective grammars as well; without a syntactic parsing of sentences we cannot give satisfaction and truth conditions. As Quine, in his inimitable way, puts it: "Logic chases truth up the tree of grammar." (Quine 1970:35).

First, we must ask whether there are analogues in English to predicates, variables, and quantifiers. A thorough discussion of this question would occupy a separate book. With regard to predicates and variables, finding their analogues would mean finding expressions in English that are purely referential and being able to conceive of an analysis of predication that would separate the referential and descriptive elements within predicates. In any case, pronouns certainly play some of the roles that variables play. The matter is much clearer when it comes to quantifiers. For it is obvious that a language like English contains a much wider variety of quantifiers than what we find in modern symbolic logic, e.g. few, many, numerous, a certain, etc. It is an open question whether these can be defined in terms of available logical apparatus. We shall see later that further difficulties arise when one considers certain combinations of these quantifiers in English.

Apart from the issue of finding analogues, there are a number of phenomena in English that this system does not seem to take care of. There are tenses, indexicals, and modifiers of various sorts that do not behave as predicates. Furthermore, there are relations of synonymy that rest on lexical meaning and not logical form that this system does not capture. Finally, there are contexts created by modal terms like necessarily and epistemic terms like believes that in which the truth value of the whole complex does not remain constant when we substitute on the basis of extensional equivalence. (For example, if all men are necessarily rational animals, and all men are featherless bipeds as well as vice versa, it does not follow that all featherless bipeds are necessarily rational animals.)

It seems that these phenomena cannot be handled in a natural way within the framework that was sketched above. Furthermore, the syntax of this system is clearly much more restricted than the syntax of a natural language. In the latter we have such categories as prepositional phrases, relative clauses, gerundives, etc., that are not represented in the logical grammar; indeed, no distinction is drawn here even between nouns, verbs, and adjectives.

These objections, however, will not seem decisive to those who are committed to the program of showing first order predicate calculus to be - under suitable interpretation - the semantic backbone of natural languages. One can handle epistemic contexts as taking sentences as their objects or as forming so many indissoluble primitive predicates, true for the believer; one can treat necessity as a primitive predicate; etc. Those who favour this program look at synonymy relations suspiciously, as not having clear behavioural criteria. With respect to the impoverished syntax, it will be said that perhaps some syntactic distinctions in a language like English do not correspond to semantic differences.

In short, except for certain phenomena to be discussed later, there is no decisive argument against such a program. But even a brief examination of these attempts shows that the treatment of the recalcitrant phenomena listed above is ad hoc, and thus seems arbitrary unless there are some independent conceptual considerations that demand that we should favour first order predicate structure above all others as a viable framework for semantic analysis. We shall review in the second chapter some of the issues that emerge in this context.

1.2.2. The Semantics of Sense and Denotation

In order to account for some of the phenomena that seem to resist natural analysis in the framework that we surveyed so far, we expand the semantics to include the Fregean dichotomy referred to above, i.e. in addition to denotation, sense will be assigned to terms. In Frege's system the assignment of intensional elements is done by keeping a fundamental cleavage between singular and general terms; in subsequent developments by Carnap and Church, this sharp distinction is dropped. Thus we can construe each denoting term as having also a sense, where this term is understood as explained in the previous sections. The senses of the various expressions contained in a declarative sentence contribute to the sense of that sentence, or the thought expressed by it. (Subsequently, for "thought" philosophers substituted the term "proposition".)

Every singular and general term has a sense, even though some of them, e.g. unicorn, might not have a denotation. Terms having the same sense must have the same denotation, but terms having the same denotation (i.e. extensionally equivalent terms) need not have the same sense.

We can now explain synonymy relations and entailments between terms as sameness of sense, or sense containment.

We can also give a more adequate account of constructions involving belief or knowledge. For the objects of belief are, on a natural interpretation, not sentences, or speech events, but propositions; what is believed and what is taken to be true or false is that which a sentence expresses. Furthermore, different (synonymous) sentences can express the same truth, and thus the same object of belief.

These observations lead to the Fregean doctrine that within belief contexts and the like, the relevant terms contained in the sentence at issue (e.g. the cat is on the mat in the context: John believes that the cat is on the mat) have indirect reference; they do not refer to (denote) what they usually refer to, but rather to what is normally their sense. This doctrine of indirect reference, and the accompanying doctrine of having intensional elements as the objects of belief, knowledge, etc., yields the view that in contexts of the sort mentioned the criteria of substitutivity will be synonymy (or, as Carnap pointed out, even finer intensional distinctions may need to be drawn).

Thus, within this Fregean framework we can account for certain data that the purely extensional system does not seem to handle in a natural way, and - as we saw from the introductory sections - we are also able to say something about linguistic competence, and not merely about how to give an interpretation to a language.

Still, even within this framework, problems remain. One of these is that we have not said much about what meanings (senses) are. To explain synonymy in terms of sameness of sense is hardly to go much beyond what we started with.

Another problem, as we saw above, is that in addition to meaning relations and opaque contexts (where extensional substitution breaks down), there were other problems that the previously considered system could not deal with. Prominent among these were the tenses and indexical expressions such as here, there, etc.

To be sure, Frege was aware of these phenomena, but his treatment of these lacks the generality and uniformity that is characteristic of the rest of his system. We shall see how subsequent developments in intensional logic were designed to remedy the situation.

We shall not review here Frege's account of truth in terms of the postulation of the two abstract entities - the true and the false - and his construal of sentences as, under certain conditions, naming one or the other. This feature of Frege's system is detachable; other accounts of truth can be added to intensional logics.

1.2.3. Possible World Semantics

The difficulties mentioned at the end of the last section, as well as the aim of extending the theory of reference as much as possible to cover semantic phenomena, led to the development of what is known today as possible world semantics. The technical developments are due to Kanger, Hintikka, Scott, Kripke, and others (for reference, see Kripke 1963). We shall restrict ourselves here to sketch in outline those aspects of the theory that are most relevant to linguistic analysis.

We saw already in the previous sections that an interpretation of a language involves considering the stock of individuals about which the language can be used to talk, and assigning these to the various predicates in the language. Looking at the whole matter in the material mode, we can consider a state of affairs that the language can be used to express as a certain configuration of particular elements and a set of properties. We can conceive of having the stock of properties (to be sure an infinite set) and then simply of taking each particular about which the language can talk and assigning to it 0 or 1 with regard to each property, depending on whether the particular has or lacks that property. Thus each particular has its own property assignments. A set of such particulars with property assignments that do not conflict with each other is a state of affairs; in fact the real world can be viewed this way.

When we plan things, desire things, consider what to believe, etc., it is essential to our tasks, as Aristotle noted, that we should be able to consider not only what is the case, but what could be or might be the case. Furthermore, we must be able to consider more than one alternative. Without these features, neither practical nor theoretical reasoning is possible. One might call this the projective aspect of the reasoning process, and possible world semantics is designed partly in order to capture this feature of natural language.

Upon the same set of particulars we can project different sets of consistent property assignments; in fact this is what we do when we plan a course of action. We consider what we take to be the actual world (i.e. particulars with property assignments) and also possible states of affairs, or possible worlds (the particulars with different property assignments). We can thus extend the theory of reference to cover not only interpretation in the actual world, but also over possible worlds. This gives us a nice way of analysing logical truths which are supposed to hold no matter what the empirical contingencies are; in short, they hold in all possible worlds. The semantics sketched here can represent this situation in a rigorous way; these truths hold under all of the consistent sets of assignments.

We also have a way of representing meanings in this semantics. We saw that the interpretation of a language over the actual world involved assigning to a predicate a class of particulars. But in this new, expanded system there are many possible worlds, and thus many assignments to any predicate. Thus we

represent the meaning of a predicate, e.g. is a man, as a function
that picks out from each possible world the set of all men. Similar analysis - but with certain complications to be treated later -
can be applied to the explication of the meanings of singular terms
as well.

Still another advantage of this referential framework is that it
gives a unified treatment not only of the modalities, but also of
tenses and indexicals. We considered so far the actual world and
possible worlds, but all of this without time references. But just
as we can - and in our ordinary reasonings do - project the actual state of affairs over possibilities, so we also project the
current state of affairs over new segments of time, or contrast
it with what happened in other segments of time; without such
processes, memory and the use of the tenses would be impossible. Thus, in addition to the actual and possible worlds, we need
to talk also about temporal worlds, or the world at certain mo-
ments of time. We can combine all of this and have as our referential system actual and possible histories of the world, thus
allowing the evaluation of statement at different points of time
(in the case of tenses, the points will be relative to that of the
speaker or intended hearer, etc.) as well as at different possible
worlds. Spatial indexicals are handled in the same way: we evalu-
ate statements containing these at different points in space relative to a hearer-speaker situation. (One can relate to this formal
system the as yet unpublished material of Charles Fillmore who
shows how in separate situations different temporal and spatial
relative references are assumed in our use of so-called "deictic"
expressions.)

In addition to these applications of the new semantics, Hintikka
has shown how its application to the epistemic modalities helps
solve some of the problems that the more traditional analyses
encountered. Perhaps the clearest exposition of this application
is Hintikka (1969).

There are at least two salient problems in the more traditional
approaches to contexts created by terms such as believe. One
difficulty with the Fregean approach was that not much is said
within that framework about what the objects of belief, knowledge,
etc., are. The other difficulty is even more directly related to
descriptive adequacy, and is shared by other, nonintensional
solutions such as Quine's. We saw that in the Fregean system
singular terms have different reference depending on whether
they occur within or outside of opaque contexts in which extensional substitution breaks down, such as that created by believe.
This leads to a certain "segregationist" policy; one cannot use a
referring expression outside the opaque context and then have
cross reference to the same thing referred to within the opaque
context. The exclusion of this sort of cross reference, called

"quantifying in", is also a mark of Quine's treatment of these
contexts, even though Quine's solution does not involve commitment to senses, thoughts, etc.

Hintikka points out that there are a number of locutions in natural languages in which the cross reference, forbidden by the traditional account, is required. These involve the knowing who
constructions as well as beliefs that an agent has about himself.
In John believes himself to be a good athlete we are talking both
about a person outside the opaque context as well as about the
same person within the opaque context, as he appears within the
belief representations.

As a solution to these problems Hintikka proposes the representation of a belief as a set of projections or possible worlds,
thus dividing the class of all possible worlds into those that are
and those that are not compatible with the belief. Thus we get the
representation of John believes that p as p holds in all possible
worlds compatible with what John believes.

We now have as the representation of a belief a set of possible
worlds compatible with a certain statement, i.e. one in which
certain particulars are assigned certain properties. In these
possible worlds, particulars occur, and clearly some particulars
occur in more than one of these possible worlds. A person holding a belief has in some cases enough knowledge so that he can
reidentify the same particulars across these possible worlds,
and then again he may lack such knowledge. Depending on whether
he has or lacks such information, he knows or does not know who
or what the objects of his belief or knowledge are. This sort of
knowledge can be represented in Hintikka's system by relating
the epistemic agent in various ways to functions that pick out the
same particular in different possible worlds. Thus within Hintikka's system adequate analysis can be given for those constructions that require cross reference, or "quantifying in" from non-
opaque to opaque contexts.

It has been pointed out that there are certain differences between logically possible worlds and belief worlds; for example,
we do not believe everything that our beliefs entail; a set of beliefs that a person holds at a given time may be an inconsistent
set without his knowing that; and that principles of individuation
may not be as clear-cut in realistic belief representations as in
possible worlds. Hintikka has made various modifications which
attempt to account for these facts.

Still, even if all of the above has been taken care of, there remain certain problems concerning possible world semantics. A
brief review of some salient ones is in order.

In order to handle the epistemic contexts, we will have to make
use not only of projections of different property assignments to
the stock of particulars in the actual world, but also of the postulation of possible entities. Some critics regard the postulation

36

of such entities as problematic. This is not a telling objection: as long as we can give principles of individuating possible entities that are as clear as the principles of individuation for actual entities, there is no good reason against such postulations.

Another, more difficult problem is raised by the fact that not only do we postulate possible worlds in this semantics, but also the same particular can be identified across possible worlds. How are we to do this? What are the essential properties of a particular that it must retain in order to remain the same across possible worlds? Philosophers attempted a variety of answers to this question, and the issue is live and unresolved as of now.

Finally, we must get back to the question whether one can represent the notion of meaning as a function on the level of predicates. But a difficulty arises which is even easier to see when we consider synonymy on the sentential level. In this framework all logical and in general all analytical truths will get the same interpretation, namely true in all possible worlds. But in lieu of further devices, this forces us to regard all analytic propositions as synonymous, a patently untenable situation: all vixens are female foxes and all bachelors are unmarried are clearly not synonymous.

1.2.4. Montague semantics

The type of theory that we surveyed in the last section has greatly expanded the referential framework within which we attempt to account for English. But as far as grammar is concerned, there has been no progress since the section in which we discussed Quine's logical grammar. To be sure, modal and epistemic operators and indices on possible and temporal worlds have been added, but the basic syntactic framework has remained that of constants, variables, predicates, and quantifiers. In the analysis of some philosophers, notably Quine, the difference between this simple syntax and that of a natural language is openly acknowledged. Quine claims that within the simple logical syntax we can represent the truths of the sciences, and that this is all that his program of regimentation is concerned with.

One salient distinguishing feature of Montague grammar (including syntax and semantics) is that it takes the syntactic categories of a natural language like English seriously. Thus in Montague grammar we find the categories of noun, verb, adverb, etc., and there is a semantic object type correlated with each such category. Indeed, since in order to show how the interpretation of a whole sentence is built up out of its parts it is necessary to subdivide the categories mentioned above, Montague has even more syntactic categories in his grammar than what one finds in a grammar book for English. Even if, say, different semantic interpretations are required for intensional and non-

intensional transitive verbs (e.g. <u>kick</u> and <u>seek</u>), the grammarian
can keep these in the same syntactic category; but it is not so
for one who is writing a grammar for a formal semantics since
the different segmentations will have to show how the different
constituents contribute in their own way to the semantics of the
whole.

Thus as a first approximation one can describe Montague
grammar as a formal semantic system operating on the same
principles as the simple "logical grammar and semantics" that
we surveyed above, except that it takes into consideration all of
the syntactic categories of natural languages, and it represents
rigorously the semantic differences, explicable in terms of entailment relations, even within these categories.

The other salient feature of Montague grammar, which is
really a consequence of the first one, is its treatment of quantifiers. In the grammar of logic, quantifiers become detached
from whatever noun phrase they qualify; thus there is no one-to-
one correspondence between a logical formula with quantifiers
and a natural parsing of an English sentence with roughly the
same semantic structure. In Montague grammar, this situation
is remedied. Quantifiers are developed within noun phrases. To
give a simplified example, let us consider the sentence:

<u>every man runs</u>

Montague assigns <u>runs</u> to the category of intransitive verbs,
and in a simplified version we can represent the semantic object
correlated as a set, i.e. the set of all those who run. He forms
<u>every man</u> as a noun phrase, and by applying <u>every</u> to <u>man</u> he
ends up assigning to the complex the semantic object of the class
of all classes that contain the class of all men. In order to check
the truth of the sentence, all one has to do is to see if the class
of all those who run is one of the classes that include the class
of all men. Analogous treatment is given to the existential quantifier in which <u>some men</u> will have as its semantic object the
class of all classes that intersect with the class of all men.

This type of analysis is developed for various fragments of
English in Montague (1970 and 1973). Montague's untimely death
prevented him from exploring the possibility of expanding the
rules so as to capture further parts of English.

It should be noted, however, that not all aspects of Montague's
analysis are equally essential to his project. As Gabbay (1973)
shows, one can present a Montague-type analysis in an intuitively
more easily graspable manner if one is willing to sacrifice some
of the elegance and uniformity in Montague's system. For example,
all noun phrases, including proper names, receive a rather complicated treatment in Montague's system because of his effort to
give uniform interpretations to noun phrases like <u>John</u>, <u>John and
Mary</u>, and <u>unicorns</u>.

38

1.2.5. Beyond Montague

Recent work in the kind of set - theoretic semantics that Montague
utilised shows that one can extend his type of analysis to certain
phenomena that he did not deal with.

   Two salient semantic phenomena, primarily connected with
nouns and noun phrases, are that we can divide those that plural-
ise from those that do not, thus denoting countable things, and
that we can attach persistence criteria to certain nouns that denote things which endure through time. Thus we can distinguish
man from earth, and we see that different criteria determine
the persistence through time of persons on the one hand, and col-
lections of body cells on the other. Recent work (Gabbay and
Moravcsik 1973) has shown that these distinctions can also be
incorporated into a set-theoretic semantics.

   Two sections ago we mentioned the problem of the tenses, and
gave a rough sketch of the kind of analysis that these would be
subjected to. Recent work (Gabbay i.p.) has shown that within a
more elaborate framework we can handle even iterated tense
references such as, for example:

she will regret that she married the man who was an officer of
the bank where she had had her checking account

   Finally, Hintikka (i.p.) has drawn attention to the presence of
so-called branching quantifier configurations in English, i.e.
configurations in which there is no linear dependency linking all
of the quantifiers of a sentence. For example:

all of the daughters of some farmers, and all of the sons of some
bankers are married to each other

The significance of these structures is that if they can be found
in English in their full variety, i.e. not just a clearly distinguish-
able subclass of these, then one should be able to prove that the
semantics of a natural language like English cannot be expressed
in the first order predicate calculus, and that the class of logical
truth in English is not recursively enumerable.

   Recent work (Gabbay and Moravcsik i.p.) shows on the one
hand that there are syntactic devices in English that make it possible to express complexities of a wide variety of branching constructions, and on the other hand, that these branching quantifiers
can be accommodated within Montague grammar.

   Further work in progress involves getting a clear set-theoretic
subclassification of different kinds of verbs (intentional, achieve-
ment, process, state, etc.), and a classification of different
kinds of adjectives and adverbs as well. In short, Montague's
work should be regarded in the following way. First, the semantics can be detached from the syntax and judged on its own merit,
as well as attached to different kinds of grammars, e.g. regular

transformational grammars. Second, Montague's suggestions about semantics should be regarded as simply one version, among the countless possible ones, of set-theoretic semantics. The success that Montague had is really the success of set-theoretic semantics in general; Montague's suggestions can be both modified and extended in order to capture larger and larger fragments of English within such a semantic theory.

1.2.6. Problems with Montague's System

So far we have seen, in rough outline, how Montague semantics operates and how one can extend it. It is time to assess the limitations of the system and to discuss the claims that Montague himself made regarding his work.

In Montague (1970:189) we find the following:

> I reject the contention that important theoretical differences exist between formal and natural languages.... I regard the construction of a theory of truth... as the basic goal of serious syntax and semantics; and the developments emanating from the Massachussetts Institute of Technology offer little promise toward that end. In the present paper I shall accordingly present a precise treatment, culminating in a theory of truth, of a formal language that I believe may be reasonably regarded as a fragment of ordinary English.

From this quotation and similar comments in Montague (1973), one may assume that Montague wished to make at least the following three main claims:

(a) His aim is to represent the semantics of a natural language like English in a rigorous and explicit way, giving truth conditions, and conditions of satisfaction in set-theoretic terms.

(b) To present the syntax and semantics of a natural language is essentially the same as the task of doing this for a formal language.

(c) Montague's semantics plus syntax is meant to have empirical content at least as much as, for example, transformational grammar is to have, and in fact is superior in some ways to the latter.

We shall consider these claims in order. The first has been discussed already in the past two sections. It is time, however, to consider some of the phenomena that, as of now, resist the kind of semantic treatment that Montague envisages.

First, we discussed already the possibility that quantifiers in English do not correspond to those in logic. Further evidence of this is provided by combinations of quantifiers illustrated in the following:

Some of the many enemies that Joe had were definitely dangerous

A combination like <u>some of the many</u> is outside of current analyses of quantifiers and cannot be treated by simply defining additional quantifiers on the basis of the ones in symbolic logic.

We have shown above how certain sentential modifiers, such as <u>necessarily</u> can be treated within a possible world semantics But there are others, such as <u>fortunately, clearly</u>, etc., that cannot be treated along analogous lines. Thus these, too, constitute phenomena with which formal semantics has not dealt adequately.

When we were considering earlier branching quantifiers, our example included prepositional phrases. Some of these can be iterated arbitrarily, e.g. <u>the dog of the daughter of the king of....</u> Prepositional phrases, however, are not dealt with in set-theoretic semantics, and it is far from clear how one would extend the system to cover these. To be sure, we can treat place adverbials like <u>in Paris</u>, but presumably an adequate semantics should be able to explain how we put together the different prepositional expressions by combining <u>in</u>, <u>of</u>, <u>for</u>, etc., with noun phrases and at times with elements from other syntactic categories.

Still another area in which problems will be encountered are comparative constructions. Even a cursory survey of Bresnan (1972) indicates that comparatives cannot be handled simply as two-place predicates or as ordering certain entities along some quantitative dimension, etc. It is quite unclear how one would give a set-theoretic analysis to a sentence like:

<u>We need a clearer analysis of semantic facts more than ever</u>

Finally, let us mention still another category for which as of now we have no adequate semantic analysis. We dealt with quantifiers and their complexities, but we have not dealt with certain uses of noun phrases in which quantifiers are absent. One of these has been named by linguists the "generic use" of certain expressions. Consider:

<u>The tiger is a four-legged animal</u>

What semantic object should be assigned to <u>the tiger</u> in this use? The statement is not about all tigers, or about the species, or about the statistical majority of tigers. It is about the normal tiger, the healthy specimen. And though such specifications are vital to biological classifications, it is quite unclear how one would represent these notions in a formal semantics.

This partial survey of phenomena that are as yet beyond set-theoretic analysis shows that Montague's claim (a) must be regarded at best as a program rather than something already accomplished.

As we consider claim (b), we must make an important distinction between two senses of formal within the phrase "formal language". In one sense this means simply that the rules can be given in an explicit, rigorous way. The denial that English is a formal language in this sense would have to amount to claiming that because of vagueness, fuzziness, etc., and because there are no clear criteria of grammaticality, the syntactic and semantic rules of a natural language like English cannot be stated in a clear and explicit way. Some of the followers of Wittgenstein and of the so-called Oxford school of analysis might make such a claim, but as of now no clear set of arguments exist that would support such a position. It is interesting to note that on this issue Montague is in complete agreement with Chomsky and the transformationalists, in spite of the harsh words that he always had for the "MIT grammarians". He might have complained that the MIT linguists did not attach a set-theoretic semantics to their grammars, but it is far from clear why one could not take the grammars "emanating from MIT" and attach to them a set-theoretic semantics of the sort Montague envisaged.

There is, however, another sense of "formal language". In the philosophic tradition we are accustomed to describe an artificial language that is constructed explicitly in order to capture a certain scientific theory (i.e. so that within it one can axiomatize a certain theory) as a formal language. Thus, given this interpretation of formal, Montague claims that English can be treated like an artificial language that we construct in order to codify a scientific theory or mathematics. Given Montague's actual work, it is quite clear that he meant to make this more controversial claim as well.

There are, however, a number of features of formal language (in this sense of formal) that natural languages lack, and vice versa. Furthermore, as we shall see, these differences cannot be treated as showing that formal languages are idealisations which natural languages approximate. The differences call for different approaches to certain tasks, and within both the work on formal languages and the work on natural languages we can posit different idealisation conditions.

First, in a formal language, such as Quine's logical grammar reviewed above, the syntax is "but a slave of semantics", to borrow Hume's phrase from a different context. That is to say, both the syntactic categories and the concatenation rules have strictly semantic motivation. Differences in semantic representation determine differentiation of syntactic categories; the formation rules are meant to provide us with syntactic units that are needed in semantic interpretation, culminating in the unit that expresses what is true or false, i.e. the sentence. Thus though the syntax and the semantics are quite distinct, the rules have different domains: one type links expressions with expressions and the other links expressions with parts of reality.

The motivation for the syntax can be found solely in the desired
semantics. There are a number of reasons to suppose that this
does not hold for natural languages. First, natural languages
are biological phenomena; thus, presumably, just as the structure of the ear and the larynx places some bounds on phonological
variety, so the structure of the perceptual and mental apparatus
presumably places some bounds on syntactic variety. In any case,
it is clear that with regard to natural languages we have empirical facts to be explained concerning what is a natural segmentation of sentences. The formal semanticist might find it con-
venient to deal with units like John loves, goes to, and helps
with, but the linguist might point to empirical facts that suggest
that this is not how we parse sentences, and that units should be
rather loves Mary, to Paris, with the dinner, etc. In short, the
syntax of a natural language requires empirical, syntactic motivation and justification. Montague seems to have overlooked
this. There are other factors that suggest independent motivation
for some of the syntax of a natural language. (Some of these are
mentioned in Ziff 1969, though he uses them to make a somewhat
different point.) For one, a natural language has a phonological
component; it is something that has to be interpreted by a perceptual apparatus. This presumably places some constraints on
it; it would account, for example, for some of those grammatical peculiarities that seem like "telescoping" from the point of
view of logical structure. (More on this in the second chapter.)
Also, as we said before, language is used, among other things,
for communication. This means that for some parts of the language - the part outside the Fregean core - one can leave much
of the semantic interpretation nonexplicit, to be supplied by
communicational contexts.

These facts help to explain why often there seems to be no
correlation between syntactic complexity and what is from the
logical point of view semantic complexity. If one considers some
of Chomsky's earliest examples, such as

The man hit the colorfull ball

it strikes one that the syntax is - at least on any natural and
theoretically prejudice-free view - relatively simple (NP plus
predicate with transitive verb and object-NP), while the semantics is complex. We have two definite descriptions, the analysis
of which is complicated; furthermore the definite descriptions
are context dependent (which man? which ball?), and we have a
past tense that requires locating the time of utterance, etc.
Needless to say, a lot of these semantic facts are, in a natural
language as used, simply left to the nonlinguistic context to sup-
ply. On the other hand, NP's with adjectives in them have a
fairly straightforward semantic interpretation, while some of
the suggestions concerning the syntax involves transformational

derivations, etc.

These considerations suggest that Montague's semantics should be detached from his conception of syntax, and that one should try to link it to other, more empirically and more independently motivated grammars.

Finally, there seems to be a difference with regard to the general conditions that constrain the semantics of formal and natural languages. With regard to the formal languages, one can characterise the domain of discourse in fairly straightforward ways. For example, in mathematics we talk about numbers, in physics about particles, in biology about the smallest units of organic life, etc. Theories usually tell us what entities they analyse and predict. But can we say anything analogous about natural languages? A natural language provides the bond or general framework within which people can discuss diametrically opposed theories about themselves and their environment. It has no clearly definable domain of individuals to talk about; presumably it does not embody a theory about the world, or else people with quite different views about the world could not be talking to each other in the same language as they obviously do.

This means that with the notions of reference, interpretation, and assignment of denotation, one might have to deal differently when considering a natural language from when considering a formal language. In the case of formal languages it is intuitively plausible to think of a "ready-made" stock of individuals that get assigned to different constants and predicates. But it is quite implausible to suggest that this is what is involved in the referential mechanism of natural languages. It is customary to contrast Aristotelian logic with modern logic by saying that the latter can account for a much larger set of inferences. What is often overlooked is another difference: in symbolic logic the referential and descriptive roles are performed by distinct elements (variables and predicates) while in Aristotelian logic the two are indissolubly fused. It is an open question as to which is a more adequate representation of natural language in this respect.

In turning to consider Montague's third claim, we have to ask what ways are provided for the empirical verification of Montague's proposals? This question leads us back to the issue, discussed earlier, of how one could ascribe the mastery of the referential structure of a language to a speaker-hearer. It is clear that any evidence provided by the verbal output of a speaker, and by inferences that he seems to make, will be related to semantic hypotheses only indirectly. Inferring is itself a mental operation, the occurrence of which manifests itself in a variety of ways in verbal and other behaviour; there can be no behaviouristic analysis of notions like proving, inferring, etc.

Perhaps Montague might have claimed that his semantic hypotheses are no more or no less closely related to empirical evidence than the hypotheses of transformational grammarians. Still, with regard to empirical applicability, there is a fact that favours the current state of syntax over the current state of semantics that Montague seems to have overlooked. One of the main results of generative grammar is the ordering of types of grammar in terms of complexity (phrase structure, context-sensitive phrase structure, transformational grammar) and the ability to associate with each type a device that will accept a language with that kind of grammar. Using this formal characterisation of grammars, one should be able to prove something about the complexity of the human mind, i.e. the device required to interpret natural languages (e.g. natural languages cannot be captured by finite state grammars). But we have no analogous ordering of semantic systems. There is currently no way in which we could order the different semantic systems by some complexity measure so as to relate the different categories to different devices. In short, with regard to syntax, we are at least in the position of seeing how characterisations of grammars could provide information about some general properties of the human mind, but semantics, including all of Montague's work, provides, as of now, no such basis.

Apart from descriptive adequacy and basis for inferences about the complexity of the mind, one might demand that semantics should have other explanatory aspects as well. We saw already that Frege introduced the notion of sense in order to capture a crucial aspect of semantic competence. Montague claimes that he was a Fregean, and that his extended theory of denotation made the sense-denotation distinction, as Frege had it, unnecessary (Montague 1970:218). Montague thinks that his representation of the meaning of a term, such as man, as a function that picks out the class of men from each possible world obviates the need for postulating an additional entity such as a Fregean sense as representing meaning. It is far from clear that Montague is right about this. The claim depends to some extent on how one interprets the notion of a function. Given an extensional interpretation, even if it is across possible worlds, a function is not equivalent to a Fregean sense. Rather, a Fregean sense is the intension that is correlated to such a function, the instructions or search procedures that under idealised conditions, determine the function. In taking seriously the opaque contexts and making these the centre of his analysis, Montague is a Fregean. In his attempt to reduce senses to functions he is not. This characterisation can be extended to just about every major philosopher of language of the past fifty years. Church and Carnap keep Frege's intension-denotation distinction, but reject the Fregean dichotomy of the object-function, complete-incomplete divisions that are for Frege grounded in the nature of things. Montague keeps some

parts of Frege's analysis of epistemic contexts but rejects
others. Even Quine is in a way a Fregean: though he tries to
eliminate intensional entities, he insists on the fundamentality
of the distinction between singular terms and general terms.
One can view Frege's theory of language as a beautiful and fra-
gile yacht that was broken up around the turn of the century.
Each major philosopher subsequently takes some, but not all,
of the broken parts and tries to make a separate ship out of it.
It does not seem that they have succeeded in constructing something that would match, in terms of scope and insight, the Fregean original.

Given that Montague himself compares his work with that of
the linguists, we should raise the question of how and to what
extent Montague's work is of help to linguists interested in semantics. At first glance, there seems to be no connection at all.
Linguists seem to be interested in finding semantic primitives
or in reducing a set of terms such as spatial prepositions to a
basic small group of concepts, and these enterprises seem independent of Montague semantics. Indeed, a linguist might claim
that in trying to understand the adverb slowly he wants to know
how it is related to the notion of speed, to other adverbs of speed,
etc., and all Montague semantics tells him is that slowly stands
for a function that takes classes carved out by verbs or verb
phrases and yields subsets of these, e.g. from those who run,
the subset of those who run slowly.

In assessing the connection between Montague's semantics and
work on semantics by contemporary linguists the latter needs to
be looked at with critical scrutiny as well. It seems that most
of what goes under the name of semantics in contemporary linguistics is really lexicography, at times under fancy new descriptions. The search for "primitives", etc., is essentially an
attempt to take, say, the Oxford English Dictionary and reduce
the vocabulary to a basic set of primitives in terms of which one
can define all of the other items. To be sure, such a task has
practical significance for a linguist, but two things should be
noted. First, there are an indefinite number of ways of doing
this sort of thing: one set of primitives for English is just as
good as another, and it literally makes no sense to ask which
one is the "real" set. Second, such work has no theoretical significance: it does not help in analysing linguistic competence, it
does not tell us what it means to understand a language, and it
provides no basis on which we could form hypotheses about the
human mind.

It is certainly true for lexicography, whatever name it goes
under today, that Montague's work as well as the work of other
writers on formal semantics is of no great help. But this is because lexicography does not tell us much about semantic competence. Formal semantics attempts to analyze semantic compe-

tence into constituents such as reference, understanding of truth conditions, understanding of the way different grammatical items such as verbs, nouns, and adverbs make different semantic contributions to a sentence, and finally, understanding how the meaning of a sentence can be understood on the basis of the meaning of its parts. These are the more fundamental problems of semantics since they show us what is involved in the mastery of a language. To these problems lexicography, the attempt to find semantic primitives and to do componential analysis, contributes little if anything. Perhaps this lies at the bottom of Montague's complaints about linguistics; he felt - and justifiably so - that linguistics has not succeeded in saying much about what constitutes semantic competence. It is clear, however, that linguists succeeded much more than Montague in specifying what syntactic competence is.

Finally, there is a further, more theoretical problem concerning the explanatory power of formal semantics. The key insight is supposed to be that we explain meaning in terms of functions that are assigned to different types of linguistic items. We gain in this way generality and a key concept which is familiar and clear from mathematics. But the generality and formal nature of the concept contains also some danger. For, given that meanings are functions, just what have we said that is significant about meanings? What is it that cannot be represented as a function? Anything, even a simple material object, can be represented as a function. Thus, unless we can put severe constraints on just what sort of functions will be admissible and what they range over, etc., we have not said anything distinctive about semantic rules. The situation is analogous to the one in syntax. It was a great advance to be able to specify grammars in terms of such notions as a transformation, but without further constraints and specifications, transformations are just Turing-machine operations. In that respect syntax and semantics are in a similar situation. Unless severely restricted, a transformation is just a series of Turing-machine operations, and becomes thus indistinguishable from any other type of rule that involves the addition, deletion, and permutation of elements. Again, unless restricted in various nontrivial ways, to say that a meaning can be represented as a function is not saying anything interesting, since just about anything can be represented by a function. Needless to say, both transformational grammar and possible world semantics have taken steps in the direction of formulating the desired specifications. But it is important to emphasize that these steps are absolutely vital to the two enterprises, and that without them formal syntax and semantics would become trivial.

1.2.7. Singular Terms

A large part of the philosophy of language of the past seventy-
five years is devoted to the discussion of singular terms. This
requires explanation. The predominant position of various naming
relations in formal semantic systems has been criticised by less
formally inclined philosophers. It has been said that philosophers
are seduced into thinking that all relations between language and
reality can be reduced to naming, or that naming is the most fundamental relation, etc. These criticisms are superficial and fail
to appreciate the central role of singular terms in any account
of what it is to understand a natural language. Part of this has
been treated above when we saw the reasons why the notion of
reference is of such central concern to Frege. We shall now
motivate further the view that the naming relation is central to
semantics. For one, it is the clearest case in which everyone
has to admit that understanding the linguistic item in question
must involve the ability to relate it to some element of nonlinguistic reality. Second, at least four fundamental issues in semantic
theory can be seen in clear light in connection with the study of
singular terms. There are the following:

(a) Are there differences between natural and formal languages
in terms of which expressions do and which do not belong to a
language? As we shall see, it is not easy to decide which singular terms belong to a language, and how they are related to other
parts of a language.

(b) Does the analysis of singular terms show the need for a
wide rift between the "logical form" of certain expressions and
their grammatical analysis? Russell, for one, thought that it
does.

(c) Is there a need for analysing the semantics of terms such
as singular terms in different ways, depending on the linguistic
context? Recent work suggests the affirmative answer.

(d) Does the class of singular terms suggest that the "Fregean
core" is smaller than Frege supposed it to be? Some recent
philosophers think that it does.

Before we look into these matters in more detail, we must
raise the issue of how one determines what are the singular
terms of a language. As an initial answer one might say: proper
names and definite descriptions. But this will hardly do as a
general characterisation. Russell (1905) thought, however, that
one can recognize singular terms only by "their form". This,
as we shall see, means that one can give only a syntactic characterisation. Thus, right at the outset, we see a striking way in
which syntax must be prior to semantic analysis. The reason
for this is the following. A singular term is designed to name
or refer to only one entity, but there is no guarantee that the
entity to which we purport to refer in fact exists. Thus there

are two reasons why one cannot say that a singular term is one
that applies only to one entity. First, because there are singular terms, e.g. a host of definite descriptions, that are well-
formed but do not happen to apply to anything (e.g. the unicorn
in my garden), and, second, because there may be a predicate
expression which happens to apply to only one thing, though it is
so designed that it could apply to many (e.g. redwood of N feet
height where we assume that there happens to be only one such
tree in the history of the world). Of course, one might try to
specify singular terms as those that are characteristically used
to refer to only one thing, but this talk about uses needs clarification. Are we making a statistical claim about the majority of
the speakers of the language? Or are we rather saying that the
rules of the language specify these terms as having such a use?
But, which rules are these? Surely, they must be syntactic rules
- classificatory rules that yield, for a language like English, as
singular terms the categories of proper names and definite descriptions.

Frege's view was, as we saw, that singular terms must have
a sense, and may or may not have a denotation. Furthermore,
in Frege's view, elaborated later by Russell, there is no sharp
difference between names and definite descriptions; the former,
in so far as it has a fixed sense, must be equivalent to a set of
the latter. Implicit in this view of Frege's is the conviction that
singular terms such as names along with definite descriptions
are parts of a natural language; thus it must be part of linguistic
competence to know what the names are used to name.

Russell's general theory of descriptions, and that special part
which became known as his theory of definite descriptions, included the claim that a proper analysis of these expressions
shows the wide rift between the parsing of sentences into the
units that a semantic analysis requires (one that exhibits conditions of truth and inferential relations) and the parsing given
by grammars of natural languages. Thus the doctrine of "logical
form" was born. We shall return to this in the second chapter
of this essay. It is important to see that Russell's criticism of
syntax is not rendered obsolete by the advent of transformational
grammar. In both new and old grammars expressions like a man
and the man will be regarded as natural syntactic units, and
Russell would object on the grounds that expressions of these
kinds do not make a distinct semantic contribution to the meanings of the sentences of which they are parts; rather, in the context of sentences, with proper analysis, a number of quite different constructions will make the semantic contributions that
we ordinarily expect these expressions to make.

Russell thought that ordinary names could be reduced to definite descriptions and Quine (1960), carrying this line of thought

further, simply eliminates singular terms in favour of predicates
on the grounds that they are not needed for a language that is
regimented so as to be lucid and be able to express the truths of
the sciences.

Such a move raises the question whether the analysis of language under regimentation (e.g. that it might serve the purposes
of science) and the analysis of a natural language, from the point
of view of what are the basic units required for communication,
coincide. Strawson (1950) argues that these analyses conflict:
though singular terms might not be needed for the natural sciences, they are certainly needed if our semantic analysis is to
reflect the basic units of language use; in this case, the units
are singular terms that are used to identify things and predicates that are used to describe that which has been identified.

The rise of the new modal logic (which we discussed informally under the heading of possible worlds semantics) brought
with it a reexamination of the analysis of singular terms. From
works like Donnellan (1966), Kaplan (1968), and Kripke (1971),
the following view emerges. One distinguishes two uses of definite descriptions in opaque contexts. One use involves referring
to an entity that happens to have a certain role in the actual
world, but might have different roles in different possible worlds,
while the other use serves to pick out under different possible
circumstances the entities that play a certain role specified by
the description in question. Names are construed as having the
same identifying force as the definite descriptions in the first,
the "de re" use, and they are claimed not to have sense - in
Frege's use of that term - but only denotation. Furthermore,
names are characterised as requiring in order to be understood by
someone a link between that person and the original event of the
name being introduced.

Let us see to what extent these different views shed light on
the four problems that we started out with. It is clear that with
regard to names, there are important differences between formal languages and natural languages. In a formal language we
have a collection of constants that we make available for being
assigned to individuals. In fact, most formal languages are designed to express theories that range over a fairly clearly definable domain. For example, in mathematics we have a systematic way of naming the various entities, and this is because
there are systematic ways of introducing the entities that mathematics is about. No wonder Frege thought that the sense-denotation distinction was not necessary in order to account for the
language of mathematics. The situation is quite different, however, when we come to natural languages. As we remarked above,
there is no way of specifying the domain of discourse: it includes
everything. Thus, likewise, there is no way of systematically

generating all of the names used. Indeed, in the typical cases, first names for persons such as John or Mary will name more than one person. The reason for this is that in a natural language the principle of least effort is at work. It is important that we should be able to distinguish all of the numbers, but it is not at all important that we should be able to tell apart all of the people in this world; as long as the people in our immediate circle of acquaintance have distinct names, no confusion is likely to result. Names originate as such local systems, and when more "global systems" are needed, then the relevant agencies, like credit-card companies, introduce a number system in place of the ordinary names.

Furthermore, it is far from clear that all names belong to some natural language. Some names do, e.g. names of the months of the year, or of the days of the week, or of numbers. But family names obviously do not. Yet ordinary names of people, pets, etc., are not just arbitrary additions to a natural language. There are only certain syntactically prescribed places where they can enter. Thus syntactically they are parts of languages, even though semantically some of them are not. Thus proper names constitute an interesting twilight zone, not found in formal languages, between what is part of a language and what is essentially a function of, to some extent, language-independent intentions of subsets of the community of language users.

With regard to our second problem, recent work on formal semantics and syntax managed to bring the analysis of definite descriptions - along Fregean lines - much closer to the usual grammatical parsings than Russell would have it. But the general issue of the relation between the two structures is still a live issue - indeed a central one in contemporary linguistics.

The need to analyse the semantics of a unit does indeed arise in connection with the semantics of singular terms. The ambiguity of definite descriptions that we noted arises only in opaque contexts - in spite of what linguists are saying about + and - readings of specificity. Furthermore, whatever plausibility the analysis of names has in logical modal contexts as designators without sense, it is lost immediately when we consider names in belief contexts and other epistemic structures.

Finally, if the analyses given by the contemporary philosophers such as Donnellan, Kaplan, and Kripke, are right, then the "Fregean core" is a lot smaller than one would have thought. For apparently, all sentences that include nonabstract proper names and definite descriptions contain some implicit link to a name giver or user and thus have an element of indexicality in them. (Indeed, this notion of "hidden indexicality" was introduced much earlier by A. W. Burks 1951.) Recently Kripke claimed that the same holds also for terms designating natural kinds. Thus the delineation of the Fregean core is a controversial issue with no clear results at this time, though no theory threatens to eliminate it entirely.

1.3. The Epistemology of Theories of Language

The type of theory that we sketched in outline, as well as alternatives in the philosophical literature, raise certain issues of knowledge and verifiability. Among these, the following three are central, and are relevant to any philosophic theory proposed in the past eighty years. First, a distinction is made between rules and regularities and the related issue of what is it to posit rules of language. This issue comes up in a particularly sharp light in the context of situations in which we posit rules to explain behaviour that suggest rule following even though there has been no conscious explicit learning. In short, the problem of positing rules to explain what looks like implicit knowledge of skills.

Second, we saw that the notion of intention plays a large role both in theories like the one outlined as well as in alternatives, e. g. in those that try to tie the concept of naming to certain intentions of the speakers of the community. The difficulty is twofold. On the one hand, we do not have a clear characterisation of the conditions under which one would ascribe intentions to an agent. Can a machine have intentions? If not, why not? It is certainly unfair to dismiss attempts to simulate the understanding of language by machines on the grounds that machines cannot have intentions unless one can make quite clear what it is that machines must possess if they are to have intentions. On the other hand, even apart from specifying what it is to have an intention, we face difficulties in cases in which it is agreed that the agent has intentions. For the question arises: how do we know the intentions of others as well as our own? Is, for example in our own case, introspection a reliable guide?

The third problem is that of the psychological reality of the competence, mastery of skills, or rule following that we posit. Does the fact that the linguist or philosopher, who constructs a theory about competence, requires the positing of rules lead to the conclusion that the agent who has the competence must have in his mind rules as well? What is the relation between the rules that the theoretician posits and the rules that are allegedly in the mind of the agent? We shall take up these matters in order to indicate where we stand today in the efforts to find solutions.

52

1.3.1. Rules, Regularities, and Tacit Knowledge

There is a tradition, exemplified by Quine (1960), of scepticism
in philosophy concerning rules. Demands are made that one
should be able to distinguish sharply rule-following behaviour
from behaviour that merely reveals patterns of regularities.
Furthermore, questions are raised concerning how one would
establish what rules an agent is following - assuming that it has
been established that his is a rule-following behaviour - especially in circumstances in which no explicit instructions have
been given to the subject.

It has been suggested, e.g. in Moravcsik (1969), that rule-
following behaviour cannot be separated from the having of intuitions of ill-formedness of moves in whatever procedure is at
issue. These intuitions are, however, themselves only indirectly
accessible; thus the connection between observation and the ascription of rule following becomes rather remote.

Quine has used the sceptical arguments to cast doubt on the
alleged semantic rules of natural languages. Certainly, even if
one would agree - as Quine no doubt would not - to the presence
of rule following where intuitions can be ascertained, in the case
of semantics it is not clear just what the relevant intuitions are.
But at the same time, we should keep in mind that the problem
of the epistemology of rules and rule following will arise in any
case with respect to other aspects of linguistic competence as
well and with respect to cognitive skills other than the use of
language. The problem arises not only with regard to semantic
competence, but also with regard to syntactic and phonological
competence. Indeed, of the three, the area in which progress
is most likely to be made is not semantics but phonology. It is
clear that phonology is constituted by rules, that a child masters
this component of linguistic competence, and that this mastery
involves an absolute minimum of explicit instruction. Since the
facts about the phonological component are more accessible than
facts about semantics, and presumably there is more opportunity
for experiment and observation, this is the area in which the
controversial concepts mentioned above should be worked out
first. Yet curiously, philosophers have practically nothing to
say about this aspect of linguistic competence; in general, arguments about rules of language tend to collapse into nebulous arguments about semantic rules.

General considerations indicate that we cannot abandon the notions of implicit knowledge and rule following completely. Let
us look at cognitive competences outside of linguistic abilities.
Every child learns how to reason, and the teaching of elementary
logic would be hopeless if one could not rely to some extent on
the students' grasp of the validity of certain inference patterns.

Does it make sense to say that rules of deductive reasoning exist only in textbooks and that no internalisation of rules underlies the reasoning competence of humans? The same considerations hold for elementary arithmetic. A child can "see" after a while that the commutative law holds for addition, even if he or she is never told. Can we account for such facts without positing implicit knowledge in such a way that this involves the internalisation of rules?

The sceptic performs an important service in calling attention to the epistemological questions, but at the same time reflection on these facts suggest that the price one would have to pay if one yielded to scepticism is much too high. Perhaps more progress can be made in answering the sceptic if one would concentrate on areas like phonology, and the reasoning ability of small children, rather than semantics and other, more complicated cognitive skills.

1.3.2. Linguistic Intentions

The mastery of the referential apparatus of a language as well as its meaning relations enables the competent speaker to form intentions of using an expression E to refer to something and to mean by a certain sequence of expressions E'...E", e.g. a certain proposition. These can be called linguistic intentions. One problem is their individuation. How do we individuate a collection of such intentions? As of now no answer is forthcoming except one that differentiates in terms of the objects of the intentions. If this is the only way, then this by itself establishes a dependency relation between the structure of language and these intentions; the rules that make up language must be conceptually prior to the intentions else the individuation of the latter could not depend on the former.

The discussion of the notion of reference in previous sections shows already that it is difficult to give criteria for when reference has taken place. It is doubly difficult to establish conditions for referential intentions. Concepts like identify, pick out, etc., cannot enter into our explanations because these themselves presuppose the notion of reference. (Or if pick out applies also to apes, then in that sense the notion will not help to explain linguistic intentions.)

Again, this set of problems should be understood against the background of the general issue of how one recognises different intentions. That we do recognise the intentions of our fellow human beings is not at issue; a sceptic at this level can be refuted in the way in which Dr. Johnson refuted the idealist. But as of now we are far from having given an adequate account of how this all-pervasive human ability is manifested and what it is made up of.

54

1.3.3. Psychological Reality

It is clear that Frege thought that certain kinds of rules are not
only the artifacts of the linguist who tries to describe a language,
but are represented in the minds of the speakers as well. Such
are the rules that one learns when one grasps what Frege calls
the sense of an expression. However, as we saw, Frege does
not say too much about these senses. When we come to more
detailed representations, such as the representation in Montague
semantics of adverbs, verbs, etc., it becomes much less clear
to what extent we can think of these representations as having
psychological reality. Still, something presumably can be in-
ferred from the nature of the representations that we produce.
For example, the relative complexity of certain semantic items,
or the dependence of larger units on smaller ones for determining
the semantic content, etc., should correspond to idealised mental
processes. It is far from clear, however, that it makes any sense
to talk about the correct semantic representation in the sense of
some unique notation and relations that would correspond exactly
to what is in the speaker-hearer's head. Again, the analogy with
deductive reasoning and mathematics is helpful. In any case,
until we have a number of adequate alternative accounts of the
semantics and syntax of a natural language, it is premature to
try to specify the relevant sense of psychological reality in detail. At present we are far from having even one adequate account of the semantics or the syntax or any one natural language.
Thus this is the top priority task, and not an attempt to antici-
pate the exact nature of the claim of psychological reality, nor
an attempt to derive some specifications of syntax or semantics
by the operation of machines that can simulate some small fragment of either semantic or syntactic competence.

1.3.4. Rationalism and Empiricism

Though sceptics concernings rules, etc., have been historically
mostly empiricists, it is important to keep these matters apart.
Anyone has to answer the questions of the sceptic in this field,
for these are legitimate questions of methodology and verifiability.
Thus the question can be raised by rationalists and empiricists
alike. Furthermore, merely saying that one is a rationalist does
not obviate the need to answer the questions.
   It is a mistake to link to rationalism or empiricism any particular formal framework within which semantics is to be done.
Formal semantics of the sort we have outlined, can be - and has
been - pursued by rationalists and empiricists alike: Frege and
Church could hardly be described as empiricists, while Russell
and Tarski clearly can be so identified. Also, the controversy
between rationalism and empiricism is often confused with contro-

versies in ontology. Thus a brief summary of the different de-
bates might not be uncalled for.

The controversies concerning the ontologies of theories of
language centre around the issue of the need for various types
of abstract entities in these theories. Needless to say, all theories admit some types of abstract entities: classes have to be
admitted by any theory, and the distinction between sentence
types and sentence tokens must be accommodated by theories of
language as well. Indeed, the need for abstract entities would
become more obvious for philosophers, and the extent of the
realm of such elements more clearly recognised, if philosophers
paid as much attention to syntax and phonology as they do to the
semantic component.

With regard to the semantic component, the controversial entities seem to be Fregean senses, meanings, intensions, and
propositions. On the one hand, the criteria of identity for these
entities as well as their relation to empirical evidence seem to
be in doubt; on the other hand, it is far from clear that an adequate theory of language can do without these elements. But the
debate between those who admit these entities, and thus have a
"Platonistic" ontology, and those who do not is not an issue of
rationalism vs. empiricism. For example, Carnap has a "Platonistic" ontology, but in his epistemology he is clearly an empiricist.

The controversy between rationalists and empiricists concerns
epistemology and the philosophy of mind. In epistemology the
issue is whether one can regard all nonempirical statements as
being analytic, i.e. true by virtue of the meanings of their constituents. This controversy affects issues in the foundations of
mathematics, as well as claims about certain incompatibilities
of colours, shapes, etc., but it has not been a main issue in the
philosophy of language. The aspect of the controversy that affects
theories about semantics can be stated with respect to one's key
assumptions about the nature of the human mind and learning.
Though both rationalists and empiricists admit that the mind is
not a tabula rasa on which sensations are imprinted, the rationalist ascribes to the human mind a rich innate structure that is
responsible for a variety of intellectual competence, whose acquisition through some clearly definable process of experience
seems implausible. Meanwhile the empiricist either restricts
himself to ascribing only innate dispositions to the human mind,
or admits a limited innate structure which is then held responsible for such general capacities as deductive and inductive
reasoning. With regard to learning, the rationalist will claim
that the notions used by empiricists, such as ostensive learning
and learning by abstraction (or inductive learning), are either
so vague as to be useless, or, when specified clearly, turn out

to be simply inapplicable to whatever we know about the learning of a language, the learning of mathematics, the learning of how to reason, etc. The empiricist, on the one hand, will rely on these allegedly unclear notions and attempt to explain the acquisition of cognitive skills in terms of them.

The debate between the two camps is only as clear as the devices that either camp claims as an explanation of the acquisition of cognitive competences. We have no way of delineating ahead of time which of all of the possible concepts of future learning theory should be classified as empiricist and which as rationalist. Thus, it can also happen that new forms of learning theories would arise that are – given the traditional predecessors – neither rationalistic nor empiricist.

Some semantic theories have developed without any regard to questions of learnability. What has been called in this part a theory of language, however, must be under the constraint that it cannot postulate semantic structures that would be impossible to learn by a human within the normal contexts. It is fair to say, however, that neither the issues between the formalists and the nonformalists, nor the differences between various versions of formal semantics reflect the distinctions between rationalists and empiricists. As of now, one could belong to either camp and still hold almost any version of current semantic theories. One hopes that as these theories gain in empirical content, one might be able to link different types of specific proposals for the semantic component to different sets of learning conditions which, in turn, would be classified according to some such scheme as rationalism and empiricism.

As a final note one should add that in this section rationalism was discussed without being identified as antimaterialistic. Historically, rationalism does not go with a materialist conception of mental and physical reality, but the issue concerning the structure of the mind in terms of what is innate as well as the issues about learning conditions can be separated within a logical analysis from the materialist-dualist controversy, and indeed such separation is desirable for the sake of clarity.

THE RELATION OF THEORIES OF
LANGUAGE TO LINGUISTICS

2.1. The Syntax of Natural Languages

The following is a clear and well-known way of introducing the
notion of a grammar for a language. Let us consider the set of
minimal syntactic units, or symbols, of a language L. Call this
set K, and then generate a new set, K*, by taking all of the possible concatenations of the elements of K. K* can be divided into
two subsets that exhaust the collection. One subset is the class
of well-formed sentences of L, and the other one the complement
class. A grammar is a device that can take K* and in a systematic way achieve the carving out of the two subsets mentioned.
In simple cases, this could be done by giving a list of the sentences. In the case of any fairly interesting language, and certainly for all natural languages, there will be sentences of arbitrary length, and thus also an infinite number of sentences. On
the assumption that there is a finite means of generating this infinite set, we postulate rules that will enable us to derive the
class of well-formed sentences and to separate these from the
other part of K*. The rules will contain a recursive element,
so that by iterated applications the same structures can be gen-
erated an arbitrary number of times. This way of characterising
a grammar assumes that there is an effective way of generating
the well-formed sequences, and that in the case of natural languages there are empirical facts that confirm or disprove hypotheses about this procedure.

   It has been said often that this effective procedure manifests
itself in intuitions about what is and what is not grammatical. It
is often assumed, however, that these intuitions are easily accessible through such techniques as question and answer. This
clearly cannot be the case. These intuitions, like most real
things, are unobservable, and responses to questions as well as
a survey of the corpus of utterances produced by a competent
speaker give indirect evidence about them. In short, people do
not wear their linguistic intuitions on their sleeves, and at present we have no carefully constructed reliable methods for making

these intuitions accessible. Current make-shift methods, like
that of asking people, have repeatedly been shown to be unre-
liable. In a recent paper Fillmore (1972:7) concludes from this
that the program of a grammar as elucidating and making explicit what underlies intuitions of grammaticality is in doubt.
This conclusion is warranted only if one identifies the intuitions
themselves with answers to loaded questions about correctness;
from a theoretical point of view such identifications are disas-
trous.

In the process of trying to elicit the intuitions about well-
formedness and constructing a grammar to account for these,
the grammarian will have to assign internal structure to the
sentences. In doing so, he must take account of the way in which
different complex expressions get parsed in the corpus, and
which ones can be used in isolation in certain circumstances. In
this sense, the structural descriptions assigned to sentences
must be natural, but this definitely does not mean that a criterion
of such "naturalness" would be what the competent speaker of
the language says about some proposed parsing. In the case of
rules of inference, we account for intuitions of validity, and in
doing so ascribe a certain logical structure to sentences, but we
do not ask the opinion of the average person on whether the proposed structure seems natural to him or her.

In all of this we talked about natural languages, and it is time
to give at least a partial characterisation of what that means.
"Natural" in this context should not be contrasted with "invented",
and certainly not with "formal". It may or may not be the case
that natural languages are formal languages, i.e. that one can
specify rigorously their syntactic and semantic structure. Again,
it may or may not be the case that an invented language like Es-
peranto could serve as a natural language.

The sense of "natural" in the theoretically interesting interpretation of the phrase "natural language" is: L is a natural
language if and only if it is a language that could be learned by
a human (or device sufficiently like a human) as a first language
under the normal learning conditions. This characterisation is
vague in certain key spots: what is a "device sufficiently like a
human"? What are the "normal learning conditions"? However,
we shall have to rely on this notion; we cannot wait until the details have been worked out. Naturalness must be tied to universal acquisition conditions. It is on the assumption that language
is partly a biological phenomenon, and that there are universal
acquisition conditions that we can talk about the general structures of language as such, in contrast to the different structures
of particular languages. It is also important that our notion of
what a natural language is should have empirical content, no
matter how vague at present.

2.1.1. Mathematical Foundations, the Formal Power of Grammars

It is commonly agreed that with the appearance of Chomsky's early work linguistics changed drastically, but the nature of the changes are not often clearly understood. In particular, it is important to sort out Chomsky's conceptual proposals and his specific empirical hypotheses. Among the conceptual proposals some are permanent contributions, regardless of further changes in empirical evidence that requires the formulation of new hypotheses about specific rules of grammar. Foremost among these permanent contributions is the provision of mathematical foundations for the theory of syntax (Chomsky 1963). To put it briefly and informally, Chomsky showed the following. First, one can specify rigorously different types of grammars in terms of such well-defined notions as that of a tree, rewrite rules, and Turing-machine operations. Grammars thus expressed can be shown to have certain formal properties, and in view of these properties we can order them in degrees of formal power. Finally, we can relate the different types of grammars to different abstract devices that would be required to accept languages with grammars of that degree of complexity. Thus one should be able to show that given certain formal properties of grammars of natural languages, no device or mind with a degree of complexity lower than a given one could comprehend natural languages. Thus it is this link between mathematics and syntax that allows us to envisage limiting proofs about the mind and about computers based on the nature of grammar. This is why there is formal as well as substantive scientific interest in constructing a grammar that not only includes all of a language like English, but only a language like English. This is also why grammars that can be specified in terms of the three types Chomsky gives - context-free phrase structure, context-sensitive phrase structure, and transformational grammars - have an initial advantage over any other rival candidate: they will have the structure that allows one to study their formal properties and thus make inferences about the complexity of the device required to accept them. This deep theoretical advantage should not be given up lightly; thus if there are proposals for other kinds of grammar, it is important to see if one could prove them to be equivalent to the three types whose formal properties have been studied. Needless to say, a grammar that is not clear enough to allow one to specify its formal properties is of no serious theoretical interest, even if it seems to a working linguist to be somehow easier to apply. In order to handle certain phenomena in a more elegant way, and to capture what seem to linguists significant empirical generalisations, Chomsky introduced the notion of a transformation. A syntactic structure for a sentence is represented by a tree structure that connects syntactic categories, and those eventually with the terminal elements that make up the string under analysis. (A real weakness of this work is that so far there are no language independent characterisations available for the various syntactic categories used by the grammarian.) A transformation is a series of operations that transform one tree into another. The operations are specified as deletion, addition, and permutation. Therein lies the effectiveness of the operations, but also therein lies the danger of too much power, and indeed vacuousness. For the operations of addition, deletion, and permutation on a tape, with unlimited back-up, etc., make up the most general characterisation of what a computation is. Thus to say that the structures of two sentences can be related by transformational operations is to say nothing unless transformations are severely restricted. A grammar with transformations that are unrestricted has too much formal power to be a significant proposal about the organisation of language. It is trivial to say that an all-purpose abstract computational device is sufficient for the understanding of natural languages, since such a device is sufficient for the understanding of any structure whose analysis involves computations.

The recognition of this point is absolutely crucial to the understanding of transformational grammar. After the initial stages when Chomsky's proposal was presented, work on syntax can be divided into two kinds. One, the theoretically sound approach, consists of finding constraints for transformations, and showing how syntactic solutions can be found within a highly constrained transformational framework. This approach characterises the work of Chomsky, Emonds, Bresnan, and others. There are three ways in which one might constrain a transformational grammar. One is to find some mathematical way of specifying that subset of additions, deletions, etc., that will be allowed to make up transformations. Though this would be the most elegant, this is also as of now the least promising way. The second way is to put empirical constraints on transformations, e.g. they must preserve certain structures, etc. This seems presently the most promising way. The third way is to constrain transformations by specifying that the sentences whose trees form the domain for the operations must be related in certain semantic ways. The most obvious but at the same time least clear constraint of this kind would be that of meaning preservation (suggested in Chomsky 1965). Apart from the fact that this leads to certain undesirable restrictions, it could only apply to transformations that relate trees that belong to well-formed sentences, since the notion of meaning preservation can be defined only as a relation between well-formed sentences. Thus, if we have a transformation that

changes a tree that is not correlated to a well-formed sentence,
then such a transformation could not be constrained by meaning
preservation. There may be other, clearer semantic relations
holding between transformationally related sentences. Work in
this direction has been done recently by Suppes (i.p.)

The other direction in which syntax moved increases the formal power of the grammar. This work, characteristic of Ross,
Lakoff, McCawley, and others, involves adding to the transformations rules that govern sequences of such operations by relating nonadjacent transformations. Such increase in the formal
power of the grammar can be shown to be in principle unnecessary, since a grammar with simple operations of addition, etc.,
must be capable of generating any language. Second, this increase in power makes it much easier to offer "solutions" but
at the price of leaving it in doubt to what extent, if any, these
"solutions" have real explanatory power. The less formal power
a grammar has, the more clear it is that a solution within its
framework has real empirical significance. This serious draw-
back of so-called "generative semantics" is often not clearly
understood. In particular, this matter will not be understood by
linguists or philosophers who ignore the mathematical foundations
of linguistics. This shows why this foundation must be clearly
grasped by anyone who has any interest in the extent to which
linguistic hypotheses have empirical content and explanatory
power. The more formal power that the rules used have, the less
clear it is whether the explanations offered have any empirical
significance and are not perhaps vacuous. If the formal power
of a grammar is increased - as when we add transformations to
the grammar - then the new operations introduced should be as
much restricted and constrained as possible.

2.1.2. Explanations and Rules in Syntax

Any discipline which addresses itself to the problem of ascribing rules to agents possessing certain cognitive competences
will be, in certain ways, different from the natural sciences,
such as physics, chemistry, etc. To be sure, the problem of
vacuousness applies to these latter branches of knowledge as
well, but the problem of generality versus vacuousness arises
in a discipline like linguistics and in one like physics in different ways. In physics we aim at lawlike generalisations, and, as
long as the concepts introduced will have some, indirect connection with observable reality, one aims at as much generality as
can be achieved. But in the case of a discipline like linguistics
- or certain branches of cognitive psychology - the aim for generality should not be confused with the ways in which the rules
attributed to agents are characterised. The most general charac-

terisation will be a vacuous one: it will simply say - in a round-about way - that the rules postulated are... rules! The less specific we are about the formal power of the rules and their empirical constraints, the less of a theory we have about the competence under study.

In these matters, generality by itself is not a priori always a desirable thing. Let us consider the issue of the alleged "faculty of language". Some researchers think that we have an all-purpose learning mechanism that enables us to master a variety of intellectual competences. Others claim that there is a special "faculty of language" that enables us to master structures that are peculiar to natural languages. The issue between the conflicting views is an empirical one. There is nothing a priori more desirable about the view that denies the existence of a faculty of language. Likewise, the issue as to how similar the mastery of the semantic component and that of the syntactic component are is an empirical question, and a unitarian theory has nothing initial in its favour. In fact, one has to be careful lest the zeal for "generality" leads one to characterise the rules to be compared on such a level of formal power (i.e. that they are operations of deletion and addition) that the claim amounts to the assertion that "rules are rules". Such generalisations should be missed at all costs!

Evidence that these matters are not fully understood by all linguists is furnished by Postal (1972:133-135) when he argues that a theory that represents all of the rules leading from semantic units to phonological representation as homogeneous is preferable to one that does not. This claim seems to rest on a confusion between what linguistics is about and what a science like physics is about. In physics we are not ascribing rule following to elements; we simply attempt to describe the behaviour of elements in lawlike fashion. Thus the question of the formal power of rules simply does not arise. A homogeneous theory is simply one which tries to account for everything by reference to the configurations and interactions of certain basic elements, e.g. at an earlier stage atoms. But a linguistic theory which is homogeneous, in the sense that it characterises all of the rules it postulates in some general terms, runs the risk of being vacuous. Sure enough, Postal says that all of the rules he postulates are transformations. He does NOT say what constraints these operations will have to obey, or whether different types of such operations, e.g. those associated with semantics vs. those with syntax, obey different types of constraints. Thus as it stands, Postal's "best theory" runs the risk of being the worst, i.e. a vacuous theory. One can say that defining a lexical item, i.e. showing what you can exchange it with, involves deletions and additions, and that transformations such as active-passive, nominalisation, etc., also involve deletions and additions. But so far we have shown nothing interesting about these components; we have said simply, that both can be characterised by the most general terms in which computations can be described. This is hardly surprising; indeed, we should reflect what it would be like if this were not true.

Perhaps another factor in the emergence of views like that of Postal is the misleading connotation of the phrase "deep structure". This is simply the pretransformational level, the syntactic representation to which transformations are to apply. There is nothing deep about deep structure! In fact, the further removed it is from surface structure, i.e. from the parsing that can be related to some empirical evidence, the less clear it is that a proper scientific hypothesis has been formulated. It is true that the more a science advances, the more its theoretical constructs become remote from observability; however, some link, no matter how indirect, must be preserved, else it becomes unclear what in principle would count as a refutation of the claim, and at that point one is no longer engaged in empirical theory construction.

There is another point at which a field like linguistics differs sharply from a natural science like physics. In the natural sciences the ability to build a model for how something works is always a gain; proving what does not work hardly counts as a great advance. The situation is completely different in fields in which we investigate the formal power of different mechanisms. Thus, on the one hand, the construction of a model for the accomplishment of certain basic human skills is hardly of great interest; such a feat by itself gives no guarantee that we found the way in which humans naturally perform the actions in question. The same performance can be reached by quite different processes and structures. On the other hand, so-called limiting proofs, i.e. arguments that show how a device of a certain degree of complexity is incapable of accepting a language with a certain set of formal properties, carry great explanatory power; it is in virtue of such arguments that we can draw some inferences about the nature of the human mind. To know that finite state grammars cannot generate a language like English is as significant as any proposal showing how a set of syntactic rules can account for a fragment of a natural language. Ideally, we should be able to formulate limiting claims about the semantic component as well, e.g. it would be interesting if instead of merely having the practical failures of machine translation, we would have a proof of why such a venture is doomed to failure.

Some of Chomsky's early work was clearly geared towards limiting proofs; a proper understanding of the significance of such results would perhaps rejuvenate efforts in linguistics and studies of computation in this direction.

2.1.3. The Myth of Pure Semantic Representation

We saw earlier in rough outline how formal semantics and syntax can work together. We need to formulate a rigorous syntax, and then assign semantic objects (such as sets or functions) to elements in the relevant syntactic categories, and then specify, as we go up the syntactic tree, how the semantic objects of the higher nodes can be derived from the objects associated with the nodes immediately below. At times linguists talk in ways that would lead to misunderstandings concerning syntax and semantics.

For example, linguists and others in the cognitive sciences talk about semantic representation or semantic structures as if it made sense to talk of semantic analysis apart from some syntactic parsing. Possibly some have been misled by the slogan according to which grammar relates sound to meaning. This slogan suggests the picture of an independent realm of semantic structures and then a set of syntactic rules that relate these to the phonological component. Such a picture is totally misleading.

Perhaps some have thought of the specification of primitives and the definitions which then relate these to all defined terms as some sort of independent structure. But the task of sorting out the primitives and providing definitions for the other terms CANNOT take place until one has determined what syntactic categories the language has available. Definitions as well as the assignment of meanings to the primitives must take into account the syntactic category in which the items in question fall. It is incoherent to think of the rules of language as starting with lexical decomposition and then somehow, via transformations, arriving at the sentences of the language. That kind of analysis would miss the syntactic categories, and thus could not contain formation rules. It could not explain what makes certain units into sentences, i.e. that which is true or false. This is the force of Quine's dictum that "logic chases truth up the tree of grammar".

Rules that explain how the complex is made up of parts are needed both for the syntax and the semantics. This is no needless duplication: we need a syntactic rule that explains how we can form from houses and red the complex noun phrase red houses; we need a corresponding semantic rule that tells us that we take the semantic object assigned to houses (e.g. the class of all houses), and the one assigned to red (on a simplified analysis, the class of all red things), and form the semantic object for red houses - the intersection of the class of houses and the class of red things.

To be sure, the same meaning may be assignable to items in different syntactic categories, e.g. in some analyses red as a

noun and as an adjective. Also, the same truth may be express-
ible by sentences with quite different internal structure (<u>Socrates
is human</u> vs. <u>humanity is exemplified by Socrates</u>). But there
are limits to the allowable variance. A language with adverbs
and adverbial expressions will require a more complicated set
of inferential links than one in which we have only nouns, verbs,
and adjectives. Again, we need certain syntactic constructions
in order to express modal propositions in a language. In short,
syntactic structure tells us what the truth-value bearing elements
of a language are, how we can form compounds of these, what
kinds of meanings can be assigned to elements given that a limited number of syntactic categories will be available, and how
one can form complex subsentential expressions that also require
semantic interpretation. Thus though we can talk of the semantic
content of a language – what truths can be expressed in it, what
meanings can be assigned to certain elements – one cannot talk
about a semantic structure or representation apart from all syntactic analyses: SOME syntactic structure must be assumed by
all characterisations of semantic content.

It is possible that those who talk about semantic representation
mean to include syntax, but only semantically motivated syntax.
An example of such a syntax is the one Quine introduces to describe the language of logic. This grammar "is designed with no
other thought than to facilitate the tracing of truth conditions"
(Quine 1970:35-36). One might call the combination of this syntax with a semantic interpretation a "semantic representation"
provided that the role of syntax is recognised. Just what the link
is between such a system and an empirically motivated syntax
for a natural language will be discussed in subsequent sections.
But this much should be noted in any case; even if one restricts
one's motives to what Quine refers to in the quotation, this leaves
us with a wide range of alternatives. For example, philosophers
have given divergent logical grammars for singular terms and
for elements in opaque contexts (i.e. intensional contexts in which
extensional substitutivity, or existential inference breaks down).
One can still ask: which of these grammars and semantic interpretations is most natural for a language like English?

Thus syntax and semantics have to be regarded as distinct
components, and the fact that one could look at lexical decomposition as a series of deletions and additions shows only that
these rules, like transformations in the syntactic component,
can be characterised by the most general set of terms used to
talk about computations of any kind. Any closer connections are
yet to be established.

2.1.4. Biological Foundations and Universals

It is by now commonplace to talk about language having biological foundations, but the literature contains hardly anything that would attempt a more careful specification of what this involves. At present, the clearest formulation seems to be: the biological structure of members of linguistic communities places some constraints on possible features, elements, structures, etc., of languages. The complete denial of this would be the claim that all of the features of languages are merely the function of the environment. Nobody would want to hold this extreme position, but claims about biological foundations are interesting only to the extent to which one can make these claims fairly specific. At this point, however, we must keep in mind the differences between the three components - the phonological, the syntactic, and the semantic. As of now, the claim of biological foundations makes clear sense only for the phonological component. There we deal with sound, and the claim boils down to saying that the phonological structure of human languages depends to some extent on the structure of the human ear and the structure of the human larynx. For example, apes cannot reproduce human language because they do not have a human larynx. (Someone might ask: "Why do they not have our larynxes?" but that is a theological rather than a scientific or philosophic issue.) Even in the case of phonology, this is largely a programmatic assertion. Just what the biological foundations for the syntactic component are is far from clear; presumably one would try to find some constraints on how the brain is organised. What is least clear at present time is the extent, if any, to which the semantic component has biological foundations. It is difficult to believe that the set of concepts that we operate with are derived from the way the parts of the brain are structured. In any case, the claim for biological foundations must be established for each of the components, and it is not clear a priori that each of the three is bound to the same extent by biological constraints.

Someone might object to this division between the three components of language. But such a sharp distinction is needed on other, practical grounds as well. From the point of view of learning and forgetting, the three components are separate, and the phonological one is the "deepest" structure, while the semantics is the most superficial. This means simply that for people who have not used their native tongue for decades, the phonology (pronounciation) is what they retain best and are least likely to make mistakes in. Next comes the grammar - they will be able to form grammatical sequences but grope for the vocabulary. Finally, what we most easily forget, and most easily learn, even at an adult stage, is the vocabulary, i.e. the semantics. Again, when it comes to learning, adults have the most trouble with the phonological part of a language, less with the grammar, and the least with the semantics. This is certainly not a matter of the semantics being similar across languages. One does not have to go to Indian languages to find difficulties: we cannot even translate ancient Greek strictly into modern English or German. There is no modern equivalent of the Greek word kalon (wrongly translated as 'beautiful'), and in the teleological conceptual framework of Aristotle and his predecessors there is no room for notions like motion or event as introduced in the post-mechanistic conceptual framework that we associate with common sense today.

This should warn us about the dangers of assuming that universals will be found on the same level across the three components. Using the distinction between substantive and formal universals (Chomsky 1965), it might be that there are substantive universals in phonology, while it may be much more difficult to establish these in syntax or semantics. We must not assume that success in finding universals in one of the three components is a reliable indication of what we will find in another.

The search for linguistic universals has intensified during the past decade, and in connection with this work a couple of cautionary remarks are in order. First, to find universals and to find something innate are not the same thing. To be sure, whatever is innate must be universal, but many universals may be simply due to environmental regularities. Each case has to be examined individually, and sorted out according to the evidence. Second, not every universal gives us some projectible property of languages. There are lawlike and nonlawlike generalisations, and thus only a subset of the universals will be such that one can postulate them counterfactually, i.e. to extend them not only to all actual but also to the (causally) possible human languages. The distinctions of innate vs. not innate, and lawlike vs. nonlawlike gives us a cross-classification. Eventually we must be able to sort out universals according to this scheme, but presently there is hardly enough empirical evidence to back up such classification of proposed universals.

2.1.5. Transformational Relatedness

It was pointed out above that transformations operate on structures defined on trees, and that it is often felt that some sort of natural relatedness should hold between sentences whose phrase markers are transformationally related. It is not clear, however, what this relatedness is. Let us start with some negative observations. It is clear that on this issue of relatedness the judgments of competent speakers are irrelevant. In other words, one cannot ask speakers of a language whether they "feel that the sentences in question are transformationally related". Such introspective judgments are of no value. Nevertheless, hypotheses about transformations presumably have implications as to mental processes; thus some behavioural evidence of speakers might be relevant.

Some of the early arguments for transformations were semantic in nature. They involved structurally ambiguous sentences and claimed that a natural way of understanding how a competent speaker can sort out the ambiguity is to suppose that the different derivations from underlying structures are part of our tacit knowledge of a language. This is a good argument; however it has been used at times to argue for something more ambitious and far less convincing, i.e. that if two sentences have the same meaning, they should be derived from the same underlying structure.

First, it is clear that such a restriction would commit one to looking for common deep structures for sentences that seem syntactically quite different. For example, the pairs

(1) The likely outcome of the struggle is John's emergence as a leader.
   It is probable that after the struggle John will emerge as a leader.

(2) She is the wisest woman in Europe.
   She is wiser than any woman in Europe.

are synonymous, but they have different syntactic structures, and there is no reason to suppose that their syntactic parsing must be derived from a common pretransformational source. Of course, given the formal power of the notion of a transformation, one can always posit a common deep structure to such pairs. But the claim that with enough deletions, additions, etc., we can get to both sentences is completely vacuous, since this would be true of any strings and the corresponding phrase markers. It is far from clear that sufficiently restricted transformations allow the positing of a common deep structure to the pairs mentioned above.

In short, the assumption that sentences with the same meaning must have the same deep structure is a dogmatic assumption without any theoretical advantages, and one that may well lead to adding unnecessary formal power to the transformational component.

In Chomsky's earlier work, SOME semantic relations held between transformationally related sentences, but not that of synonymy. One might take the Fregean notion of a thought or proposition as basic, and think of sentences derived by operations on propositions (negation, questions, etc.) as transformationally related to the original declarative.

In short, there is no preestablished rigid criterion that tells us which sentences must be transformationally related. One must see how the grammar works out, and which types of restricted transformations would actually simplify the syntax. Only after such a survey can one say anything specific about the nature of relatedness. At that point, however, not anything goes: one must be able to give arguments to show why it is reasonable to posit such relations as part of the competence of a fluent speaker.

If this is right, this shows once more that a detailed consideration of semantic relations is not a prerequisite for working out the syntax of a natural language.

2.2. The Syntax of Natural and Artificial Languages

We assume that the general form of syntax will involve phrase markers and transformations defined on structures of trees. It was argued above why one should stick to such a standard presentation of syntax; only within this framework does one have clear understanding of the formal properties of grammars. The semantics will be defined either on the pretransformational or the posttransformational phrase marker, or partly this way and partly that way. The choices that present themselves at this point are of no great theoretical importance.

We saw above that in the case of grammars for artificial languages, languages that are designed to express some theory, the syntax is simply tailor-made to the semantics: one introduces syntactic categories to mark semantic distinctions and to trace truth conditions. There are, however, several general considerations to indicate that this will not be true of the syntax of natural languages. The following three conditions differentiate natural languages from artificial ones in such a way that one would expect the difference to show up in the way the syntax is organised.

First, natural languages are used for person-to-person communication. This places premium on brevity and perceptual perspicuity, and it allows much to be left implicit, to be supplied from assumed background information.

Second, natural languages have biological foundations. This suggests that there may be a variety of constraints on the form of grammars that are quite independent of semantic considerations.

The fact that a natural language is used for communication and is partly biologically determined suggests also the possibility that a natural syntactic parsing will be determined by functional units: as suggested by Strawson, certain units of language are needed in order to identify things, describe things, etc. These functional units often do not coincide with the units created by a syntax that is designed only to make explicit truth conditions. It is an empirical question whether some syntactic categories in natural languages might not correspond more to functional units than to the units of a purely logical grammar. This is how one might explain the importance of the subject-predicate distinction in the grammars of natural languages and the absence of this distinction in most purely logical grammars.

Third, natural languages are historical phenomena. Thus issues of change of meaning, accidental innovation, evolution of new uses, etc., are relevant to descriptions of natural languages, while they are obviously – and rightly – ignored when one treats an artificial language. Again, one would suppose that general syntactic structure would be affected by this difference; the syntax of a natural language must be such as to make change, evolution, etc., possible in certain relatively smooth ways. No such constraints apply to purely logical languages.

Needless to say, this is only a general way of indicating these differences. But this is the foundation for suggestions toward further research to find actual examples that show how these factors make part of the syntax independent of semantic considerations.

Finally, unlike in the case of artificial languages, we must consider empirical, syntactic evidence when we formulate hypotheses about the grammar of natural languages. The categories as well as the rules must be partly syntactically motivated. This is the sort of evidence that philosophers and logicians never consider – again, correctly – when dealing with artificial, formal languages that are created to express a given theory. Since such evidence is foreign to those working in formal semantics, a brief review of some examples might be in order.

2.2.1. Syntactic Evidence

The notion of syntactic evidence can be divided into two parts: on the one hand, certain facts need to be explained that philosophers never consider, and on the other hand, certain facts determine partially what can count as natural syntactic parsing and these facts are independent of semantic considerations.

The following are examples of facts that need explaining in a syntax for natural languages (these have been selected from Bresnan 1972). In writing a grammar that has rules for particles like than, as, that, and for, one of the facts that a linguist wants to explain is that these are clause initial in English. This is, of course, quite independent of any truth conditions, but is the sort of fact that a syntax for English cannot ignore. Again, when considering the analysis of sentences containing pretty often, one has to account for the fact that Sally eats the stuff pretty often is well formed, while Sally eats pretty often the stuff is not. This is a syntactic fact, but working out the truth conditions for the sentence would leave such issues untouched.

When analysing constructions containing <u>enough</u> and <u>much</u>, certain syntactic regularities have to be explained, e.g. what they can modify, etc. One must explain also why <u>enough</u> does not go with elements like <u>so</u>, or <u>as</u>, while <u>much</u> does. One might argue that this latter fact can be accounted for on semantic grounds. <u>So</u> and <u>as</u> will joint with quantity words to form quantitative comparisons on some projected scale, but although <u>enough</u> characterises quantities, it does not place a quantity on a scale. Its role is to indicate that a quantity has met certain presupposed standards. The point is, however, that a proper grammar for English has to capture the generalisations that express the syntactic similarities between <u>enough</u> and <u>much</u>, while in the analysis of an artificial or purely logical language such data does not arise.

As a final illustration, there is the fact that <u>no</u> but not <u>not</u> can occur in contexts like <u>... more reliable a man could be found</u>. This is the sort of fact whose explanation would not arise as a task in the construction of a logical grammar.

As an illustration of natural parsing, let us consider a sentence like <u>he goes to Paris</u>. From the point of view of semantic interpretation it is quite reasonable to suggest that we parse this as (<u>he</u>) (<u>goes to</u>) (<u>Paris</u>). We could then define relational predicates such as <u>goes to</u>, <u>comes in</u>, <u>gives for</u>, etc., and give the obvious semantics. But there is empirical evidence that this is not the natural parsing: we add adverbial material between the verb and the preposition, and not between the preposition and the verb. This is seen in <u>he goes</u> (happily, slowly, etc.) <u>to Paris</u> in contrast to the ungrammaticality of <u>he goes to</u> (happily, slowly, etc.) <u>Paris</u>. From the point of view of logical semantics there is no reason why "goings to", and "comings from", etc. could not be "sad", "happy", "slow", etc., but syntactically this simply will not do. That leaves us with the problem of having <u>to Paris</u>, <u>from the outside</u>, etc., as constituents, and it is far from clear how these should be given a set-theoretic interpretation. This issue appears in different ways depending on the structure of specific natural languages. In ancient Greek, the prepositions can combine with certain verbs, and in other languages like Hungarian some of what are prepositions in English are expressed by suffixes. These possibilities give different natural parsings, and there is not the slightest reason to believe that underlying such variety of constructions there must be a common semantically motivated "deep structure" from which all of these will be derived. Again, if we allow unrestricted transformations, the claim that such a structure exists becomes trivial and vacuous. A good grammar will account for ALL of the facts, and many of these in the case of natural languages are independent of logical and semantic considerations.

2.2.2. Logical Form

As we saw, an adequate theory of truth and satisfaction for a
language shows us how to construct larger units out of parts;
thus such a theory gives us a syntax for certain parts of the
language. As Quine notes in the quotation given earlier, this is
a purely logically motivated grammar. In the structures gener-
ated, some elements such as quantifiers and connectives are
purely logical elements. Some of the structure depends solely
on these elements; this part of structure can be called the logical form of sentences. As G. Harman (1973:75) puts it: "The
logical form of a sentence is that part of its structure that involves logical elements." As defined, logical form is a clear
notion with limited relevance to the analysis of a whole natural
language. Unfortunately, the notion has been used in a variety
of ways, and even when it is clear how a writer uses the relevant term, there are differences of opinion concerning logical
form and its relation to the grammar of natural languages.

First, logical form, as defined above, must be distinguished
from prescriptive notions such as regimented form as used by
Quine. In Quine (1960) sentences are given certain regimented
forms, but the aim there is to pay attention only to those aspects
of language that are relevant for the employment of language to
express truths of sciences. This regimentation should not be
confused with the idealisation conditions postulated in linguistics; needless to say, Quine himself is most careful in observing
these distinctions.

Second, logical form as defined above is distinct from the
kind of functional basic semantic form that is discussed in the
writings of philosophers like Strawson. In Strawson (1950) we
find an acknowledgement that Russell was right in his analysis
of what the truth conditions are for statements with definite descriptions as subjects, but that he did not bring out what the
basic units of such sentences are in terms of which one can explain the key uses of language, such as referring, identifying,
etc. It is clear why a logically motivated grammar and Strawson's
analysis have to differ for natural languages. For in a use like
the identifying use of certain expressions the referential and
descriptive roles are inextricably intertwined, while in logical
notation the two are kept sharply distinct: the variables have the
purely referential role while all of the descriptive power is built
into the predicates which, with the variables, can be used to
build open sentences.

Having made these preliminary distinctions, let us examine
the nature of logical form. As Harman (1972:39) remarks, a
theory of logical form must "account for all obvious implications
in the language". We can take, however, the notion of obvious
implication in a narrower or a wider sense. (Harman himself

discusses this difference on the following page.) In the narrower sense, it will include only the logical truths, i.e. those truths that depend on logical form alone. In the wider sense, it will include the logical truths and those truths that depend on meaning postulates, or sense assignments. E. g. "if x is a bachelor, then x is unmarried" is an "obvious implication" in the wider sense, but not in the narrower sense.

Given this characterisation of logical form, it should be clear that a variety of different proposals for logical form can be made concerning a given set of sentences. There is no such thing as THE logical form of a certain type of sentence: there is only A logical form, given a certain analysis. This is obvious in the case of singular terms where Russell's analysis competes with that of Frege, or in the case of adverbs that can be construed as predicates of events or as functions operating on the semantic objects of verbs or adjectives. This pluralism of logical form was already mentioned in 2.1.3. above; it is emphasised by such writers as Grandy, Harman, and Quine, but the point is not always appreciated by linguists.

An appreciation of the plurality of viable analyses should help one in becoming sceptical about claims to the effect that the same logical form can be found in the sentence types of all natural languages; in other words, that there is some common logical structure underlying the surface forms of all natural languages. Scepticism is expressed in Harman (1973); in general, it is far from clear what would count as empirical evidence in deciding the correctness of such a hypothesis. Of course, one could always decide to write grammar in that way, but in that case many of the transformations would be totally without syntactic motivation, and furthermore, the transformations to be used would most likely not be of a restricted sort. But, as we saw above, any move that would increase the formal power of the grammar needlessly should be avoided. The only universality that is theoretically desirable, and in fact seems quite plausible, is that the logical forms of sentences in various natural languages should be constructible within the same general logical framework, but not that the different languages should have the same logical form. (The analogous point for syntax is that all languages have a transformational component, and the transformations are constrained in the same way, but different languages have quite different transformations.)

One may place various constraints on one's view of acceptable logical form. One of these is that the proposed form should be compatible with obvious facts about language acquisition and language use. This is, of course, not a constraint that a logician as such would accept, but it is necessary for any proposal that is to become part of a semantic theory about natural languages.

Thus, the proposal should not introduce an infinite number of primitives or even an indefinitely large number of complexes that will have to be regarded as semantically primitive.

Another possible constraint is the requirement that logical form should remain as close to the surface parsing of sentences as possible. Whether one accepts this constraint will depend on one's view about transformations and about the basis for our hypotheses about surface parsing. In this paper the point of view adopted involved wanting to minimise transformations, and claiming that there is independent empirical evidence about "natural surface parsing". Given such considerations, the constraint discussed here recommends itself.

Various other constraints have been proposed. In Harman (1972) it is proposed that logical form should not deviate more than necessary from standard logic (by which apparently first order predicate calculus is meant), and that the ascription of ontological commitment to those using the language should be kept to a minimum. These constraints rest on views about the nature of logic, conceptual frameworks, etc., and we cannot deal with all of these matters here. It will suffice to point out simply that according to another coherent point of view there is nothing privileged about first order predicate calculus; if keeping close to surface form requires the use of higher order logics and possible worlds semantics, then such employment is deemed on this alternative view desirable (see the discussion of the previous constraint). Furthermore, it is a matter of dispute just what economy in ontologies amounts to. In a sense, a theory that has propositions as bearers of truth value is more economical than a theory that has sentences in that role. Certain forms of Platonism may be more economical than certain forms of nominalism, etc.

Given that one makes one's choices with regard to logical form, what else do we need to take account of when considering the semantic structure of a natural language? As mentioned above, one might ask that certain functional units, basic for the use of language, be accounted for. One might also demand that the illocutionary force of various utterance types - at least in cases in which this force is explicit, and there are syntactic correlates - should also be accounted for. Finally, there are arguments showing that such grammatical relations as subject-predicates are also relevant to semantic interpretation, e.g. S. Anderson (1971). Evidence for the latter are sentences with verbs like <u>swarm</u> - the <u>garden was swarming with bees</u> vs. <u>bees were swarming in the garden</u>. Again generic sentences seem to support this thesis, e.g. <u>the tiger lives in India</u> vs. <u>India contains the tiger</u> (the latter is hardly well-formed, and <u>India has tigers</u> is not synonymous with first sentence). Thus it is far from clear

that logical form, even in the wider sense, is all that is relevant
to representing the semantics of a natural language.

When it comes to determining whether logically motivated syntax would be suitable for "deep structure", or simply for the
pretransformational level, we must keep in mind that this syntax governs only those elements of the language that make a contribution to truth value. Clearly, there are lots of other elements
as well (however, alas, there is in some cases, where we speak
of there insertion, etc.). Thus at most, the logical syntax could
be a part of the pretransformational level.

We saw in the earlier sections that the syntax of natural languages is determined by factors other than merely the demand of
semantic interpretation. This is one of the key respects in which
a natural language differs from artificial languages. This suggests
that in order to get the simplest and most (formally) constrained
grammar, it might be desirable to have as the pretransformational structure something other than the logical syntax. In any
case, it is an open and empirical issue whether logical syntax
could fill the bill; a priori there is nothing desirable about a
theory within which logical syntax has this role.

This leads us to the consideration of the relation between the
construction of logical syntax and the grammarian's task of
writing a well-motivated syntax for a language. Harman (1972:
63,65) objects to possible world semantics on the grounds that
it can be accommodated by just about any syntax that the grammarian might come up with. It does not place - in Harman's
view - sufficient constraints on an acceptable syntax; thus it
does not aid the linguist.

One might, however, on the basis of some of the considerations adduced in this paper, turn around the matter, and claim
that what Harman perceives as a shortcoming is really a virtue.
For it is not clear that the semantics is supposed to put constraints on the syntax - why not the other way around?

It has been argued above that the syntax of a natural language
is determined by a number of factors in addition to semantics.
Furthermore, there is independent empirical evidence concerning what are natural categories and what are natural parsings.
Thus there are semantics-independent criteria for judging the
syntactic proposals concerning natural languages, and there are
semantics-independent facts that a good syntax has to account
for.

These considerations suggest that it is the syntax that should
act as a constraint on the various proposals for logical form.
Viewed in this context, the fact that a possible world semantics
can be made compatible with a variety of different syntactic
structures counts in favour of such a semantics rather than
against it.

We can thus formulate the following program: one should take
an empirically and syntactically motivated grammar and see to
what extent one can write a sound possible world semantics for
it. Neither the syntax nor the semantics is sacrosanct; if irrec-
oncilable differences develop, one might have to modify both.
Formal semantics is thus an aid to the linguist, for though it
does not act as much of a constraint on the form of the grammar,
it accounts for some of the salient facts that the linguist will
characterise as "semantic", and it shows the grammarian how
the meaning of whole structures can be formed from the parts,
as well as accounting for differences in the meanings of sentences.

2.2.3. Autonomy of Syntax

Previously, we argued against the myth of pure semantic representation, thus showing that semantic analysis is not autonomous: it cannot be treated in total isolation from syntax. In the
last section we considered ways in which the syntax is independent. It is time to review the various ways in which syntax can
be said to be independent of semantics; confusions concerning
the various types of possible autonomy have led to much misunderstanding in linguistics and philosophy of language.
   There is a basic and minimal sense in which syntax is independent of semantics within the systems we considered under
the label of formal semantics. That is to say, in such a system
syntax is simply distinct from semantics. The domain for syntactic rules is that of expressions; the rules of syntax shows how
one can form larger syntactic units from more basic elements.
Semantic rules have the role of associating semantic objects
with syntactic categories and with expressions within these categories, as well as showing how the semantic object associated
with a larger unit can be built up out of the semantic objects associated with parts. Even if on the basis of such work we can define certain relations between expressions such as synonymy or
entailment, these relations are indirect; they are based on the
relations that the relevant expressions have to semantic objects.
It is simply incoherent within such a system to talk about there
not being a sharp line between semantics and syntax.
   On the basis of the above, one can see that syntactic rules
must be also distinct from that part of semantics that is dealt
with in a dictionary; i.e. the decomposition of lexical items. The
basis of such decompositions lies in the relationships between
certain phrases and certain semantic objects - synonymous expressions are linked with the same semantic object. To be sure,
both lexical decomposition rules and syntactic rules are rules,
so are the rules of arithmetic, but the domains are different,

and the empirical evidence relevant to the assessment of the respective hypotheses will be quite different for the two types of cases.

Syntax can be regarded as autonomous in a stronger sense if it could be shown that one can define the basic set of syntactic categories not only across natural languages, but also in a semantics-independent way. The first rudimentary attempts in Western thought to define some basic syntactic categories were made by Aristotle. They were attempts to define the categories semantically in terms of what sorts of things the items in the respective categories designated, and the efforts resulted in failure. There is a real lacuna in current syntactic work concerning the definitions of the basic categories. If adequate definitions for "verb", "noun", etc., that do not rely on semantic or functional notions would be forthcoming, then the claim for autonomy would be that much stronger.

There is a third sense in which one may regard syntax as autonomous; this is the sense that we discussed when we attempted to show how natural languages differ from artificial ones. That is to say, autonomy in the context of this claim amounts to saying that a number of syntactic rules are quite independent of any semantic motivation and rest on independent evidence.

This is the kind of autonomy that is claimed in the early writings of Chomsky, and in this essay attempts were made to strengthen the argument for this. That elegance and simplicity within a purely syntactic analysis does not coincide with logical form is clear from the early transformational work. The most impressive parts, such as Chomsky's treatment of the auxiliaries, were precisely those that had no relation to any obvious semantic interpretation. One can argue further for this type of autonomy on the basis that without some semantics-independent constraints on the (humanly) possible form of grammars language acquisition becomes impossible to account for.

There are certain salient facts about the semantics of natural languages that separate this component from syntax. One of these is vagueness; while it can be argued that vagueness in the denotation range of certain terms is useful for language change and is also a result of the "principle of least effort", there is no analogous aspect of syntax. The syntactic role of an expression cannot be described as "vague".

Again, much of the semantic interpretation of a natural language takes place against the background of certain general assumptions, e.g. regularities in nature, certain general categorisation, etc. None of these seems to affect the syntax; whether we should use nouns, adverbs, etc., does not depend on general assumptions about the world we live in.

To be sure, what sounds odd or peculiar depends on assumptions about the world, but this shows only the need for remembering a distinction emphasised in Chomsky's early work between grammaticality and interpretability. No matter how difficult it is to come up with clear empirical criteria by which one can establish intuitions of ungrammaticality, we know that this notion must be distinct from that of interpretability. To say that one can assign a semantic interpretation to an ill-formed sequence is to say that one can assign with reasonable probability an interpretation that corresponds to what was intended by the speaker. In other words, when we interpret something ill-formed, we do not simply look at the language, but consider psychological evidence about the speaker - something that we need not do in the case of the well-formed sequences. The judgment of grammaticality, on the other hand, does not require knowledge about the state of mind of the agent who produced the utterance. What is or is not grammatical are types of expressions, while what can be interpreted, even though it is not grammatical, is a token in a given context.

With regard to the interpretability of natural languages, there is another point in favour of possible worlds semantics, and against a semantics within first order predicate calculus. Unlike an artificial language, a natural language allows interpretability only within certain limits set by background assumptions about the universe. For example, the rules of the language tell us what an animal is only on the assumption that living things have continuous existence; given a world in which things go in and out of existence at various times, and return randomly, our rules for terms like animal simply do not apply, and we would not know what to say about the creatures in such a world. This fact about natural languages can be well represented in a possible world semantics; for we simply limit the function that picks out the denotation classes for animal to those possible worlds in which the background assumptions hold. Thus, when considering all of the logically possible worlds, the meaning functions of a natural language will be only partial functions; the limitations are themselves truths holding in certain worlds, and thus can be represented clearly in such a semantics.

2.2.4. Semantics in Linguistics

Though much is being written about semantics today by linguists, judged by the usual criteria of what it takes to produce a theory in a science, one can say without prejudice that at present there exist no theories of semantics in linguistics or in any of the other social sciences. A brief review of the kind of work done and a brief comparison to some philosophic work might be in order.

Much of recent and current work in semantics, e.g. so-called componential analysis, is concerned with lexicography. Such work has obviously limited theoretical interest. There are many different ways of reducing the vocabulary of a language to a set of primitives, and there is no reason to regard any one of these as psychologically basic. Furthermore, whatever empirical evidence is available - even just within Indo-European languages - speaks strongly against the possibility of "universal lexicography", i.e. the claim that one could find a set of basic primitives for the vocabulary of all natural languages. One cannot, without loss of meaning, translate the vocabulary of people who do not live in a society that has a mechanistic, post-Newtonian conception of the universe into the vocabulary of people who think within such a framework. (Which is not to say that we cannot learn and understand what it is like to think in the other framework.)

Some years ago a proposal emerged that became linked to developments in generative grammar, even though there is no logical entailment between the latter and this proposal. This is the proposal of Fodor and Katz in terms of semantic markers and distinguishers. The following are reasons against regarding this proposal as a genuine empirical theory. First, the obvious epistemological problems concerning markers and readings - What it is to know one of these? How one can tell whether a creature possesses the right concepts? etc. - are not treated anywhere. Second, it is not clear how one would test the predictions: if one could only test the predictions on subjects who have to know the vocabulary of the theory - analyticity, readings, etc. - then we do not have a bona fide hypothesis. Third, unlike formal semantics, this proposal does not show in clear, formally intelligible terms how one composes the semantic objects of the complexes out of the parts. Reference to amalgamation will not help unless this is tied to a system like formal semantics in which grammatical categories are related to set-theoretic objects. Finally, in order to recast this into a genuine theory one would have to divorce it from nebulous claims about semantic markers being universal, language independent, etc. In short, at best and in a considerably changed form, this proposal could be made into the equivalent of a part of a Fregean theory of formal semantics.

There are a variety of suggestions concerning semantic information in the literature linked to the label of "generative semantics". In order to assess how much, if any, of this material could be worked into the shape of a genuine empirical theory, one would have to sort out the following factors: (a) what is information that is not about the rules of language but about the psychology of the speaker (e.g. if someone says that he regrets being poor, then I know that he thinks that he is poor, but this

80

is information about the speaker, not about the language);
(b) what is material that can be incorporated into a formal semantic framework; and (c) what is other relevant information
about how one performs certain acts that involve language use,
and how is the use of language tied to the existence of certain
institutions (marriage, law, etc.). At best, the current literature
in this area shows that there are facts to be considered that formal semantics has not taken account of. It is far from clear that
a theory of language - in contrast to theories about communicational skills, etc. - must account for all of these facts.

The most interesting material in the linguistic literature is
to be found in the writings of Charles Fillmore (e.g. Fillmore
1969) who gives evidence with regard to the analysis of come
and go that the philosophical notion of indexicality needs to be
refined to account for natural language, and who provides evidence from verbs of judging that the illocutionary force of certain expressions needs to be referred to in certain natural ways
of representing differences of meaning. Whether one needs all
of Fillmore's proposed apparatus (presuppositions, cases, etc.)
is far from clear, but the data presented in his writings will
have to be dealt with by any adequate formal semantics for natural
languages.

It is instructive to compare Fillmore's interest in illocutionary
force with an earlier presentation of Urmson (1952). Urmson
calls attention to "parenthetical verbs", and points to pairs like:

I believe that this is Mr. Livingston
Mr. Livingston, I believe

Urmson points out that the parenthetical use of verbs can be
understood as an attempt by the speaker to call attention to the
logical relevance or the credibility of what is being said. This
sort of explanation of use clearly covers what is part of linguistic competence, yet it is not codified within formal semantics.
We can see here also a nice example of the difference between
natural and formalised artificial languages. There would be no
parenthetical verb uses in an artificial language, for such a
language is not used for communication person-to-person; thus
the issue of giving warrants, etc., for what is said does not
arise.

The examples Urmson gives, as well as the one above, are
also interesting because the shifting positions of the I believe or
I suppose are just the sort of thing that could be explained naturally by the introduction of transformations. Yet it is equally
clear that such transformations would not be meaning preserving.
This, I believe, is Tom's coat, and I believe that this is Tom's
coat do not have the same meaning. The latter could be challen-
ged on the ground that the speaker does not really have such a

belief, while the former does not assert the existence of such a belief, and is thus not open to that sort of challenge; indeed the full semantic force of the former cannot be fully given in terms of truth conditions.

2.3. Psychological Reality of Rules

We surveyed various types of rules that are needed to account for the semantics and syntax of a natural language. It was pointed out also that this work is designed to account for linguistic competence. Thus the question arises: what is the relation between the linguistic competence of the speaker-hearer and the set of rules that the linguist or logician postulates to account for the language? According to one view, the set of rules postulated do no more than account for the set of well-formed formulae, thus representing the ability of the competent speaker-hearer. There is no direct link between the rules postulated by the linguist and whatever it is that accounts for the linguistic ability of the speaker-hearer. According to the other view, linguistic competence is to be accounted for by hypothesising that the speaker has internalised a set of rules. Thus what the rules of the linguist are supposed to do is not only generate the well-formed sequences, but also represent the rules that the speaker knows tacitly and in virtue of which he can interpret the well-formed sequences. According to the first view, the rules that the linguist posits have no psychological reality, while according to the second view they should aim at representing rules that do have psychological reality.

It must be remembered that we are talking about linguistic competence, and not performance. To claim in this context that grammatical rules have psychological reality is not to claim that in actual performance speakers go through the kinds of derivations that the linguist postulates. All kinds of shortcuts, semantic information, "heuristics" in the form of probabilistic hypotheses about the environment and sequences of formulae, etc., make actual performance in most cases much easier. One could, however, rely on the ability to relate syntactic structures and to interpret these in the absence of other clues. In short, just as in the case of arithmetic we do not go through all of the proofs required for certain conclusions even though we could see that such proofs underlie what we take to be correct, so in the case of language, even though one does not go through derivations, etc., in everyday life, what one knows can be represented as going through such derivations under idealised conditions.

The issue of psychological reality arises with regard to each of the components. In the case of syntax, the parsing and the

transformational rules are claimed to have psychological reality,
while in the case of semantics it is the functions yielding the
semantics, as well as possibly the lexicographical decompositions.
The latter might enter more directly into performance. If one
could show that in terms of reaction time the interpretation of
two equally long, equally often used, logically equivalent phrases
differs, then one might argue that the speaker regards one of the
two more fundamental and interprets the other derivatively. The
same considerations hold for the phonological component.

Claims of psychological reality can be divided into two types.
On the one hand, someone might claim that the rules postulated
correspond exactly to those that the subject internalised. It is
fair to say that current knowledge about linguistic competence
has not reached the stage at which such ambitious claims could
be given much support. The other type of claim about psychological reality has to do not with the specific rules, but with the
type of rules postulated (e.g. in terms of complexity). One might
argue that though we do not know what rules the competent
speaker of English has internalised, the evidence is strong
enough to show that these rules must be phrase-structure rules
and transformations. Claims of this sort give us powerful hypotheses about the human mind; if one can be sure that the human
mind is the sort of entity that deals with operations on the level
of formal power such as a transformation, this would give us far
deeper characterisation of what the mind is than what is emerg-
ing presently from the social sciences such as psychology and
sociology. Similar considerations apply to semantics. This explains why it is so desirable to try to arrive at a characterisation of semantics that would give us degrees of complexity like
the syntactic models do. As of now, the most that one could claim
is that a competent speaker's tacit knowledge can be represented
by the kinds of functions that are employed in current possible
worlds semantics.

2.3.1. Innateness

Given the facts of normal language acquisition and the claim of
psychological reality discussed above, it is reasonable to suppose that an innate structure underlies our tacit knowledge of
the rules of language. If one denies psychological reality to rules
and denies the existence of an innate structure, one must take
linguistic competence, i.e. a set of dispositions or abilities (the
latter being a special subset of dispositions), as basic. But this
leaves one with a puzzle: how can we take a dispositional property, like being flexible as basic without inquiring into what structure of constituents results in the object having this disposition?
In general, all of the sciences assume that dispositional properties must be explained eventually by reference to the structure

of elements, or the interaction of these with the environment, of the entities to which the disposition is ascribed. This notion goes back to Aristotle; he thought that all potentialities of substances must be accounted for by reference to the form and the matter of the substances involved.

This line of thought is the basis for the innateness hypothesis in its most general form. It states that there must be an innate structure that accounts for the states of having internalised certain rules; and these states are partly what accounts for our linguistic abilities.

At this point the question arises: innate structures of what? Ideas, processes, etc.? At this stage of our knowledge, it is difficult to answer what the innate structures have to be like, and besides, it is not as if notions like that of an idea were clear. Thus there is not much point in discussing whether the innateness hypothesis about language is committed to innate ideas. It is committed to there being mental structures that place strong constraints on the acquisition device, and thus correspond to the strong constraints that limit drastically the class of possible grammars and semantic organisations (as a subset of the class of logically possible grammars and semantic systems). The innate structures thus postulated are not at all on the level of items like the idea of redness, or that of being a man. Rather, they correspond in ways not yet specifiable to organisational principles of syntax and semantics. Furthermore, the innate structure is not activated except at certain stages of maturation, and given certain necessary environmental conditions; in this respect the innate mental mechanism is not different from what we usually describe as the physical one (there is nothing in this proposal that would prevent us eventually from identifying the mental and the physical).

One might ask at this point whether, given the vagueness of the hypothesis, the assumptions about innateness are of any use or of any empirical significance at all? Though specific proposals cannot be worked out yet at this stage, the hypothesis is significant because its provisional acceptance reorients lines of research. Instead of trying to account for verbal performance piecemeal, and then attempting to generalise by "analogy", etc., the hypothesis suggests that one should attempt to form hypotheses about the structure of what is acquired or mastered, and then try to see how specific are the proposals one can form on the basis of such claims about the nature and organisation of the human mind. This line of thought should lead us to determine whether the innate structures postulated to account for linguistic competence are specific to this particular competence or are so general as to include all skills that involve reasoning. Again, knowing this much about the human mind would give us far more

important and fundamental knowledge than what is achieved by
attempts to simulate limited fragments of certain competences
where there is no assurance whatever that the way we simulate
what is accomplished corresponds at all to the way in which humans perform those activities naturally.

2.3.2. Epistemology Again

In the previous sections claims about tacit knowledge and the
innateness of some of this was motivated. This raises epistemological problems. What is it to have tacit knowledge? How do
we know when someone has tacit knowledge of something? The
notion of tacit knowledge does not fit the categories of modern
epistemology; within this framework one distinguished between
propositional knowledge and know-how as the only epistemic
categories. Propositional knowledge is on the conscious level,
know-how need not be. Tacit knowledge is clearly not propositional knowledge by the characterisation given above, and at the
same time, it is not mere know-how, i.e. a mere set of dispositions to perform in certain ways. The fact that tacit knowledge
does not fit the modern epistemological categories should not
cause concern. These categories have been shaped by a tradition
that was heavily influenced by empiricism. The notion of tacit
knowledge has a fine tradition in rationalist philosophy; the first
philosopher to postulate tacit knowledge was Plato in his discussions of learning where this process is likened to recollec-
tion.

There is a need to develop a modern epistemology within which
more categories of knowledge can be accommodated. It is a mistake, however, to look at semantics as the field with regard to
which new epistemic notions can be developed with relative ease.
Concerning semantic competence, it is difficult to draw the line
between rule and habit, between the dictionary and the encyclo-
pedia. The field that would serve ideally as data for new epistemological concepts is the one that philosophers look at least
frequently, namely phonology. In the case of phonology there
can be no argument about the fact that children follow rules and
that the rules have not been consciously acquired. Also, one cannot argue that it is difficult to separate knowledge of these rules
and extraneous information about the world, etc. Furthermore,
the physical facts are relatively clear. Such work, however,
would require that philosophers delve into linguistics much
deeper than they have done so far.

3

CONCLUSIONS

3.1. On Semantics

One of the most important tasks of the immediate future is to
see how far we can extend possible worlds semantics to capture
the kinds of more subtle semantic distinctions that the Oxford
philosophers and linguists like Fillmore are good at pointing
out.
    At the same time, we must keep in mind that not all of the
meaning structures of a natural language can be given within a
framework that has truth and reference at its core. Thus a second task is to see how one can graft unto the core of formal semantics an account of the semantics of those elements of language
whose understanding is not centered on truth and reference (illocutionary force, nondeclaratives, etc.).
    The further exploration of possible worlds semantics must be
conducted with an open mind; it may be that further work, e.g.
on comparatives or prepositional phrases, will show conclus-
ively the limits for semantics of this approach or of any other
approach that is within the general framework of formal semantics.
    Thus, while we extend the possible worlds analyses, one should
keep an eye out for possible alternative approaches to semantics.
At present the only vaguely promising approaches might be either
to borrow from intuitionism in the foundation of mathematics and
to develop some sort of constructionist semantics for natural
languages, or to take the notion of a language game and try to
make it both more rigorous and formally intelligible as well as
show how it can be used to explain the semantic details of different types of expressions in natural languages.
    In all of these explorations attention must be given to the prob-
lem of tying down these approaches to semantics to empirical
criteria and procedures of indirect verifiability. In the course
of paying attention to this urgent task, one will have to spell out
exactly what the idealisation conditions are for a semantic theory, and thus for semantic competence. We have given evidence

in this essay to show that semantic, syntactic, and phonological competence can be separated, not only in theory, but also in observational terms (forgetting, relearning, etc.).

Another, really fundamental issue for the semantics of the near future is the determination of what exactly is left of the "Fregean core", as it was called in this essay. Is it only the category of proper names that lies outside of it - strictly speaking a subset of proper names - or do the exceptions include names for natural kinds, artifact terms, etc.? Recent attacks on the Fregean core suggest that this core might be so small as to make it not the central part of semantics. The issue is, however, far from settled. Nor is it clear how we are to represent that part of the semantics that lies outside of the Fregean core. We had success with spatial indexicals and tenses within the possible worlds framework; what is one to do about names and general terms designating natural or artificial kinds?

As was shown above, it is important to consider ways of formalisation when one considers analyses of different parts of the semantics, because only through more precise formalisations will we be able to reach the point at which we will be able to argue from the structure of the semantic component to some general partial characterisation of the human mind - something that the framework provided by Chomsky already allows us to begin in the case of syntax.

The issue of Fregean core vs. what lies outside of it cannot be made into a matter of idealisation. If the understanding of large segments of a natural language requires us to be linked somehow to certain name givers, or to certain privileged events of discovery, etc., then this is just as true of the idealised speaker-hearer as it is of us.

Finally, the issue of lexicography vs. formal semantics should be laid to rest. Obviously, we need both. If linguists did not work on dictionaries, we would not know much about all the different languages and translation would not be possible. On the other hand, it must be recognised that merely knowing what is in a dictionary will not tell us how combinations of words give us larger semantic units, and what the conditions are for the truths of various sentences of the language. Finally, lexicography, even if we had for comparison all of the dictionaries of all natural languages, cannot show anything interesting about the organisation of the human mind. Though at present the same must be said of formal semantics, in the case of the latter it is at least possible in principle that further developments should give us the required structures and basis for inference.

3.2. On Syntax

One of the most pressing needs is to push through an effort to
define the syntactic categories, or to see to what extent language-
independent definitions are feasible. It will be also interesting
to see to what extent such definitions do or do not rely on semantic or functional notions.

Second, it is important to push ahead with syntactic analyses
of parts of natural languages that are framed within a highly restricted transformational network. One cannot emphasize enough
the need to work with as clear and as stringent restrictions on
transformations as possible, and that any increase in the formal
power of a grammar should be undertaken only as a last resort.
In particular, there seems to be at present no need for the kind
of increase in power as adopted by generative semantics. In its
use of a formally less restricted framework with its ad hoc rules,
generative semantics has over the restricted Chomsky-type
grammar all of the advantages of theft over honest toil.

Third, one would hope for further progress in mathematical
linguistics. After the early successes of defining degrees of
complexity and the corresponding automata, this fundamental
branch of linguistics has not continued to yield exciting results.
Yet the ideal situation would be if one could define a device that
can accept the grammars of natural languages and that is on the
one hand more powerful than the devices defined for different
phrase-structure type grammars and on the other hand is less
strong than a Turing machine.

Finally, in this essay various arguments have been advanced
to show that the grammars of natural languages are determined
by factors other than semantics or functional matters. Thus
there is no reason to think of a syntax that is to a large extent
independent of semantic considerations as arbitrary.

To think that every syntactic distinction must mirror some
semantic or functional difference is to fall victim to "naive and
extreme Darwinism". This would amount to assuming that all
of the syntax must mirror something that is useful for us in communication, analogous to a belief that every feature of a biological organism can be explained in terms of principles of adap-
tation. Needless to say, Darwin never held such a view, and no
respectable biologist would try to account for the fact that we
have five fingers instead of six or four, or for the length of our
spinal cord, by referring to the "survival of the fittest". There
is no empirical evidence for such extreme means-ends relations
in linguistics, and thus both on theoretic as well as on empirical
grounds this sort of "naive and extreme Darwinism" should be
rejected. To ask about function and purpose sooner or later leads
one to theological questions, and these are clearly outside of the

domain of linguistics or any other science.

In general, a science is much more likely to make progress, especially in its initial stages, if the facts to be concerned with and accounted for are described in a narrow way. As long as physics was "philosophy of nature" and tried to account for everything linked to material objects and their interactions, it made little progress beyond general wonderment. Once the subject was narrowed down to phenomena like mass, motion, velocity, etc., much more rapid progress was possible. Today everything connected with verbal behaviour is in danger of being shoved into linguistics. This can only harm the subject. Progress lies in the direction of rigorous accounts of clearly and narrowly defined sets of phenomena. Such concentration does not prevent a science from building powerful and abstract explanatory frameworks. It is better to have a clear conceptual framework within which sound explanations can be given for a narrow range of phenomena than to start with the task of explaining everything that seems related to verbal behaviour. In this respect linguists might study with profit the history of the natural sciences.

3.3. Syntax and Semantics

When philosophers look at the task of constructing a grammar they are likely to concentrate on representations that are most economical, given certain semantic aims. In short, the syntax is determined by considerations of what might be the best way to represent semantic facts. There are tendencies in the same direction in linguistics. On the one hand, the so-called generative semanticists want to start with some sort of semantic representation and have the syntactic organisation dependent on that, while some linguists talk of "logically based" grammars that resemble, at least in deep structure, the grammars of logical calculi.

The proposal that emerges from this essay is diametrically opposed to these conceptions. It starts by justifying the claim that in the case of natural languages there is good reason to suppose that syntax is determined by factors other than semantic and functional considerations, and that there is independent empirical evidence about correct parsing, structural relatedness, etc. The proposal then consists of taking such independently motivated grammars, and trying to work out for these possible world semantics. To be sure, the possibility of having to modify either syntax or semantics when the two are joined must be left open, but the program at least would be to affect a union as much as possible by leaving the two frameworks intact.

Of all of those in existence today, such a theory would have the best claim to approximating a realistic representation of human linguistic competence as far as the semantic and syntactic components are concerned. It would be tied to empirical considerations both on the syntactic side, and on the semantic side, the latter in terms of predicting the proper inferences. Hopefully, in the long run one would be able to raise questions of formal complexity and associated automata – be they physical or mathematical abstractions – about such systems.

It is most unlikely that the program proposed here will be popular. For it is far more difficult to do syntax in a formally restricted and not semantically motivated framework than it is when we allow ourselves rules of all sorts other than restricted transformations. Again, it is far easier to do semantics on a syntax that is tailor-made for that purpose than on one which has independent motivations and empirical constraints. The more difficult, however, is also often the more satisfying theoretically, and never has that been more true than in this case.

The aim of such a system is to attempt to capture what is unique about human linguistic competence. In this respect there is perfect agreement between Chomsky and Frege. Both look at syntax and semantics from this point of view. There is a contrast between this view and the one often adopted both by those who favour a logically based grammar and those working in artificial intelligence, according to which it is sufficient to build a system that will include in what it can analyse the class of natural languages. This brings us back to the issue whether or not the structure of language can show something about the structure of the mind. If one wants to prepare the ground for that kind of inference, then the Frege-Chomsky view becomes imperative. Indeed, this is a point of view that underlies the whole rationalist tradition from Plato onwards. Plato believed that one cannot know the contents of the mind directly; thus one has to find a way to view intellectual competences, e.g. arithmetic, in such a way that one should be able to infer from our abilities in these fields something about how our minds are organised.

3.4. What Linguistics and Philosophy Can Do for Each Other

In recent years there has been a growing exchange between philosophers and linguists. Philosophers expected at times that new techniques of studying the structure of language will solve some of their traditional problems, while linguists expected that studying logic and philosophy will help to solve vexing problems in syntax, especially the syntax of quantifiers, pronominalisation, etc.

While exchange between fields is always desirable, one must not overestimate the extent to which linguistics and philosophy can help each other. Some of the expectations were no doubt fed by the "grass is greener on the other side of the fence" attitude which tempts one when faced with difficult problems.

On the one hand it is clear that studying what the linguist discovers about our uses of words like know, true, exist, etc., will not help to solve traditional problems of epistemology and metaphysics, nor will it show these problems to be pseudo-issues.

On the other hand it is equally clear that nothing in his professional training and activities renders a philosopher competent to write grammars for natural languages. If one wants to do competent work in syntax, one needs thorough training in linguistics; knowing logic or philosophy will not help. This may sound like a trivial observation, but in the light of current developments it is worth making.

The linguist concerned with semantics should learn logic and formal semantics, and see how far the latter needs to be modified to be tied to empirical facts and fitted to syntax. At the same time, the work of the linguist is of interest to the philosopher, for it - especially phonology - provides data for the construction of new epistemological notions, and new theories of mind and mental abilities. Studying what linguistics can do in the generative framework helps to see the problem about rules and rule following in a new perspective.

It is, of course, always useful for a scientist to be concerned with philosophical issues, and for philosophers to be concerned with conceptual problems and issues of methodology within some given science. On these matters linguists and philosophers can cooperate, but the link is no stronger between linguistics and philosophy than between philosophy and any of the other sciences.

Transformational grammar and formal semantics have been subjected at recent conferences and in as yet unpublished papers to attacks from those sympathetic to artificial intelligence projects and to efforts to achieve quick and practical results in psychology. The charge is that we have not been able to tie these disciplines sufficiently closely to empirical data and practical application. Such charges are, unfortunately, all too familiar. The tragedy of the development of the social sciences has been all along the constant heavy pressure to be practical and to yield quick applications. Such pressures cause enormous harm to a science; one wonders where the physical sciences would be today if they had not been allowed to develop in theoretically interesting ways for a long time prior to the rise of technology. In this context it is good for linguistics to be oriented towards philosophy and mathematics, for these disciplines represent disinterested theoretical understanding: the emphasis is on knowledge and not on control. In trying to divert linguistics from developing theoretical frameworks without much concern with practical application, the critics are putting the cart before the horse. Again, some attention to the history of the natural sciences might be of some therapeutic value here.

Undoubtedly some of the concerns of the philosopher with meaning will be taken over by the linguist as his science too becomes independent and goes its own separate way. But the notions of truth and understanding are of perennial theoretical interest; no doubt philosophers will find new "residual problems", and their labours - like those of Sisyphus - will never cease.

BIBLIOGRAPHY

Alston, William P.
  1964 Philosophy of Language (Englewood Cliffs:Prentice Hall).
Anderson, S.
  1971 "On the Role of Deep Structure in Semantic Interpret-
      ation", Foundations of Language 7, 387-396.
Bresnan, Joan W.
  1964 "Theory of Complementation in English Syntax", unpub-
      lished dissertation (MIT).
Burks, Arthur W.
  1951 "A Theory of Proper Names", Philosophical Studies 2,
      36-45.
Chomsky, Noam
  1963 "Formal Properties of Grammars", in P. Luce, R. Bush,
      and E. Galanther (eds.), Handbook in Mathematical Psy-
      chology 2 (New York: Wiley), 323-418.
  1965 Aspects of the Theory of Syntax (Cambridge: MIT Press).
  1972 Language and Mind, enlarged ed. (New York: Harcourt,
      Brace, Jovanovich).
Davidson, Donald
  1967 "Truth and Meaning", Synthese 17, 304-323.
Donnellan, Keith
  1966 "Reference and Definite Descriptions", Philosophical
      Review 75, 281-304.
Fillmore, Charles
  1969 "Types of Lexical Information", Foundations of Language
      10, supplem. (Dordrecht: Reidel).
  1970 "On Deixis", mimeo., University of California, Berkeley.
  1972 "On Generativity", in S. Peters (ed.), Goals of Linguistic
      Theory (Englewood Cliffs: Prentice Hall), 1-20.
Fodor, J., and J. Katz
  1963 "The Structure of a Semantic Theory", in J. Fodor and
      J. Katz (eds.), The Structure of Language, 479-518.
Frege, Gottlob
  1892 Philosophical Writings, edited by M. Black and P. Geach
      (New York: Humanities Press, 1952).

Gabbay, Dov
1973 "Representation of the Montague Semantics", in Hintikka
et al. (eds.), Approach to Natural Languages (Dordrecht:
Reidel), 395-409.
1974 "The Treatment of Tenses in English", in J. Moravcsik
(ed.), Logic and Philosophy for Linguists (The Hague:
Mouton).
Gabbay, Dov, and J. Moravcsik
1973 "Sameness and Individuation", Journal of Philosophy 70,
513-526.
1974 "Branching Quantifiers, English, and Montague Grammar", Theoretical Linguistics.
Harman, Gilbert
1972 "Logical Form", Foundations of Language 9, 38-65.
1973 Thought (Princeton: Princeton University Press).
Harrison, Bernard
1972 Meaning and Structure (New York: Harper and Row).
Hintikka, Jaakko
1969 "Semantics For Propositional Attitudes", in J. W. Davis,
et al. (eds.), Philosophical Logic (Dordrecht: Reidel),
22-45.
1974 "Branching Quantifiers". Linguistic Inquiry.
Hintikka, Jaakko, et al. (eds.)
1973 Approach to Natural Languages (Dordrecht: Reidel).
Kaplan, David
1968 "Quantifying In", Synthese 19, 178-214.
1973 "Bob and Carol and Ted and Alice", in Hintikka, et al.
(eds.), Approach to Natural Languages (Dordrecht:
Reidel), 490-518.
Kripke, Saul
1963 "Semantical Considerations on Modal Logic", Acta
Filosofica Fennica 16, 83-94.
1971 "Identity and Necessity", in M. Munitz (ed.), Identity
and Individuation (New York: New York University Press),
135-164.
Lakoff, George
i.p. "On Generative Semantics".
Montague, Richard
1970 "English as a Formal Language", in B. Visentini, et al.
(eds.), Linguaggi: nella societa e nella tecnica (Milan:
Edizioni di Communita), 189-222.
1973 "The Proper Treatment of Quantification in Ordinary
English", in Hintikka, et al. (eds.), Approach to Natural
Languages (Dordrecht: Reidel), 212-243.
Moravcsik, Julius M.
1965 "The Analytic and the Nonempirical", Journal of Philosophy 62, 415-430.

94

1969 "Competence, Creativity, and Innateness", Philosophical
       Forum N.S. 1, 407-437.
1974 "Linguistics and Philosophy", in Sebeok (ed.), Current
       Trends in Linguistics 12 (The Hague: Mouton).
Peters, Stanley (ed.)
1972 Goals of Linguistic Theory (Englewood Cliffs: Prentice-
       Hall).
Postal, Paul
1972 "The Best Theory", in S. Peters (ed.), Goals of Linguis-
       tic Theory (Englewood Cliffs: Prentice-Hall), 131-170.
Quine, Willard V.O.
1953 From the Logical Point of View (Cambridge: Harvard
       University).
1960 Word and Object (New York: Wiley).
1970 Philosophy of Logic (Englewood Cliffs: Prentice-Hall).
Rogers, Robert
1963 "A Survey of Formal Semantics", Synthese 15, 17-56.
Russell, Bertrand
1905 "On Denoting", Mind 14.
Strawson, Peter F.
1950 "On Referring", Mind 59, 320-344.
Suppes, Patrick C.
i.p. "Congruence of Meaning", Proceedings of the American
       Philosophical Association 1973.
Tarski, Alfred
1936 "The Concept of Truth in Formalized Languages", Logic,
       Semantics, Metamathematics (Oxford: Oxford University
       Press), 152-278. Reprinted in 1956.
Urmson, J.O.
1952 "Parenthetical Verbs", Mind 61, 480-496.
Winograd, Terry
1971 "Procedures as a Representation for Data in a Computer
       Program for Understanding Natural Language", MIT
       Project MAC TR 84 (Cambridge, Mass.: MIT).
Ziff, Paul
1969 "Natural and Formal Languages", in S. Hook (ed.),
       Language and Philosophy (New York: New York Univer-
       sity Press), 223-240.

INDEX

LIBRARY OF DAVIDSON COLLEGE

Books on regular loan may be checked out for **two weeks.** Books must be presented at the Circulation Desk in order to be renewed.

A fine is charged after date due.

Special books are subject to special regulations at the discretion of library staff.